POEMS

AND

ESSAYS

JOHN

CROWE

RANSOM

VINTAGE

BOOKS

A DIVISION OF

RANDOM HOUSE

NEW YORK

POEMS

AND

ESSAYS

SELECTED,

EDITED,

AND

ARRANGED BY

THE AUTHOR

JOHN

CROWE

RANSOM

CONTENTS

POEMS

ESSAYS

POEMS

JOHN

CROWE

RANSOM

WINTER REMEMBERED

Two evils, monstrous either one apart,
Possessed me, and were long and loath at going:
A cry of Absence, Absence, in the heart,
And in the wood the furious winter blowing.

Think not, when fire was bright upon my bricks,
And past the tight boards hardly a wind could enter,
I glowed like them, the simple burning sticks,
Far from my cause, my proper heat and center.

Better to walk forth in the frozen air
And wash my wound in the snows; that would be
    healing;
Because my heart would throb less painful there,
Being caked with cold, and past the smart of feeling.

And where I walked, the murderous winter blast
Would have this body bowed, these eyeballs streaming,
And though I think this heart's blood froze not fast
It ran too small to spare one drop for dreaming.

Dear love, these fingers that had known your touch,
And tied our separate forces first together,
Were ten poor idiot fingers not worth much,
Ten frozen parsnips hanging in the weather.

MIRIAM TAZEWELL

When Miriam Tazewell heard the tempest bursting
And his wrathy whips across the sky drawn crackling
She stuffed her ears for fright like a young thing
And with heart full of the flowers took to weeping.

But the earth shook dry his old back in good season,
He had weathered storms that drenched him deep as
   this one,
And the sun, Miriam, ascended to his dominion,
The storm was withered against his empyrean.

After the storm she went forth with skirts kilted
To see in the strong sun her lawn deflowered,
Her tulip, iris, peony strung and pelted,
Pots of geranium spilled and the stalks naked.

The spring transpired in that year with no flowers
But the regular stars went busily on their courses,
Suppers and cards were calendared, and some bridals,
And the birds demurely sang in the bitten poplars.

To Miriam Tazewell the whole world was villain
To prosper when the fragile babes were fallen,
And not to unstop her own storm and be maudlin,
For weeks she went untidy, she went sullen.

The little cousin is dead, by foul subtraction,
A green bough from Virginia's aged tree,
And none of the county kin like the transaction,
Nor some of the world of outer dark, like me.

A boy not beautiful, nor good, nor clever,
A black cloud full of storms too hot for keeping,
A sword beneath his mother's heart—yet never
Woman bewept her babe as this is weeping.

A pig with a pasty face, so I had said,
Squealing for cookies, kinned by poor pretense
With a noble house. But the little man quite dead,
I see the forbears' antique lineaments.

The elder men have strode by the box of death
To the wide flag porch, and muttering low send round
The bruit of the day. O friendly waste of breath!
Their hearts are hurt with a deep dynastic wound.

He was pale and little, the foolish neighbors say;
The first-fruits, saith the Preacher, the Lord hath
    taken;
But this was the old tree's late branch wrenched away,
Grieving the sapless limbs, the shorn and shaken.

By night they haunted a thicket of April mist,
Out of that black ground suddenly come to birth,
Else angels lost in each other and fallen on earth.
Lovers they knew they were, but why unclasped, un-
  kissed?
Why should two lovers go frozen apart in fear?
And yet they were, they were.

Over the shredding of an April blossom
Scarcely her fingers touched him, quick with care,
Yet of evasions even she made a snare.
The heart was bold that clanged within her bosom,
The moment perfect, the time stopped for them,
Still her face turned from him.

Strong were the batteries of the April night
And the stealthy emanations of the field;
Should the walls of her prison undefended yield
And open her treasure to the first clamorous knight?
"This is the mad moon, and shall I surrender all?
If he but ask it I shall."

And gesturing largely to the moon of Easter,
Mincing his steps and swishing the jubilant grass.
Beheading some field-flowers that had come to pass,
He had reduced his tributaries faster
Had not considerations pinched his heart
Unfitly for his art.

"Am I reeling with the sap of April like a drunkard?
Blessed is he that taketh this richest of cities;
But it is so stainless the sack were a thousand pities.
This is that marble fortress not to be conquered,
Lest its white peace in the black flame turn to tinder
And an unutterable cinder."

They passed me once in April, in the mist.
No other season is it when one walks and discovers
Two tall and wandering, like spectral lovers,
White in the season's moon-gold and amethyst,
Who touch their quick fingers fluttering like a bird
Whose songs shall never be heard.

The friar had said his paternosters duly
And scourged his limbs, and afterwards would have
   slept;
But with much riddling his head became unruly,
He arose, from the quiet monastery he crept.

Dawn lightened the place where the battle had been
   won.
The people were dead—it is easy he thought to die—
These dead remained, but the living all were gone,
Gone with the wailing trumps of victory.

The dead men wore no raiment against the air,
Bartholomew's men had spoiled them where they fell;
In defeat the heroes' bodies were whitely bare,
The field was white like meads of asphodel.

Not all were white; some gory and fabulous
Whom the sword had pierced and then the grey wolf
   eaten;
But the brother reasoned that heroes' flesh was thus.
Flesh fails, and the postured bones lie weather-beaten.

The lords of chivalry lay prone and shattered.
The gentle and the bodyguard of yeomen;
Bartholomew's stroke went home—but little it mat-
   tered,
Bartholomew went to be stricken of other foemen.

Beneath the blue ogive of the firmament
Was a dead warrior, clutching whose mighty knees
Was a leman, who with her flame had warmed his tent,
For him enduring all men's pleasantries.

Close by the sable stream that purged the plain
Lay the white stallion and his rider thrown,
The great beast had spilled there his little brain,
And the little groin of the knight was spilled by a
stone.

The youth possessed him then of a crooked blade
Deep in the belly of a lugubrious wight;
He fingered it well, and it was cunningly made;
But strange apparatus was it for a Carmelite.

Then he sat upon a hill and bowed his head
As under a riddle, and in a deep surmise
So still that he likened himself unto those dead
Whom the kites of Heaven solicited with sweet cries.

BELLS FOR JOHN WHITESIDE'S DAUGHTER

There was such speed in her little body,
 And such lightness in her footfall,
It is no wonder her brown study
Astonishes us all.

Her wars were bruited in our high window.
We looked among orchard trees and beyond
Where she took arms against her shadow,
Or harried unto the pond

The lazy geese, like a snow cloud
Dripping their snow on the green grass,
Tricking and stopping, sleepy and proud,
Who cried in goose, Alas,

For the tireless heart within the little
Lady with rod that made them rise
From their noon apple-dreams and scuttle
Goose-fashion under the skies!

But now go the bells, and we are ready,
In one house we are sternly stopped
To say we are vexed at her brown study,
Lying so primly propped.

THE TALL GIRL

The Queens of Hell had lissome necks to crane
At the tall girl approaching with long tread
And, when she was caught up even with them,
    nodded:
"If the young miss with gold hair might not disdain,
We would esteem her company over the plain,
To profit us all where the dogs will be out barking,
And we'll go by the windows where the young men
    are working
And tomorrow we will all come home again."

But the Queen of Heaven on the other side of the road
In the likeness, I hear, of a plain motherly woman
Made a wry face, despite it was so common
To be worsted by the smooth ladies of Hell,
And crisped her sweet tongue: "This never will come
    to good!
Just an old woman, my pet, that wishes you well."

Fleet ships encountering on the high seas
Who speak, and then unto the vast diverge,
These hailed each other, poised on the loud surge
Of one of Mrs. Grundy's Tuesday teas,
Nor trimmed one sail to baffle the driving breeze.
A macaroon absorbed all her emotion;
His hue was ashy but an effect of ocean;
They exchanged the nautical technicalities.

It was only a nothing or so, and thus they parted.
Away they sailed, most certainly bound for port,
So seaworthy one felt they could not sink;
Still there was a tremor shook them, I should think,
Beautiful timbers fit for storm and sport
And unto miserly merchant hulks converted.

We shall come tomorrow morning, who were not to
have her love,
We shall bring no face of envy but a gift of praise and
lilies
To the stately ceremonial we are not the heroes of.

Let the sisters now attend her, who are red-eyed, who
are wroth;
They were younger, she was finer, for they wearied of
the waiting
And they married them to merchants, being unbe-
lievers both.

I was dapper when I dangled in my pepper-and-salt;
We were only local beauties, and we beautifully
trusted
If the proud one had to tarry we would have her by
default.

But right across her threshold has her Grizzled Baron
come;
Let them wrap her as a princess, who'd go softly down
a stairway
And seal her to the stranger for his castle in the gloom.

If there was a broken whispering by night
It was an image of the coward heart,
But the white dawn assures them how to part—
Stoics are born on the cold glitter of light,
And with the morning star lovers take flight.
Say then your parting; and most dry should you drain
Your lips of their wine, your eyes of the frantic rain,
Till these be as the barren cenobite.

And then? O dear Sir, stumbling down the street,
Continue, till you come to wars and wounds;
Beat the air, Madam, till your house-clock sounds;
And if no Lethe flows beneath your casement,
And when ten years have not brought full effacement,
Philosophy was wrong, and you may meet.

VAUNTING OAK

He is a tower unleaning. But how will he not break,
If Heaven asault him with full wind and sleet,
And what uproar tall trees concumbent make!

More than a hundred years, more than a hundred feet
Naked he rears against the cold skies eruptive;
Only his temporal twigs are unsure of seat,

And the frail leaves of a season, which are susceptive
Of the mad humors of wind, and turn and flee
In panic round the stem on which they are captive.

Now a certain heart, too young and mortally
Linked with an unbeliever of bitter blood,
Observed, as an eminent witness of life, the tree,

And exulted, wrapped in a phantasy of good:
"Be the great oak for its long winterings
Our love's symbol, better than the summer's brood."

Then the venerable oak, delivered of his pangs,
Put forth profuse his green banners of peace
And testified to her with innumerable tongues.

And what but she fetch me up to the steep place
Where the oak vaunted? A flat where birdsong flew
Had to be traversed; and a quick populace

Of daisies, and yellow kinds; and here she knew,
Who had been instructed of much mortality,
Better than brag in this distraught purlieu.

Above the little and their dusty tombs was he
Standing, sheer on his hill, not much soiled over
By the knobs and broken boughs of an old tree,

And she murmured, "Established, you see him there!
    forever."
But, that her pitiful error be undone,
I knocked on his house loudly, a sorrowing lover,

And drew forth like a funeral a hollow tone.
"The old gentleman," I grieved, "holds gallantly,
But before our joy shall have lapsed, even, will be
    gone."

I knocked more sternly, and his dolorous cry
Boomed till its loud reverberance outsounded
The singing of bees; or the coward birds that fly

Otherwhere with their songs when summer is sped,
And if they stayed would perish miserably;
Or the tears of a girl remembering her dread.

THE SWARTHY ONE—
Villagers who gather round,
This is Fides, my lean hound.
Bring your bristled village curs
To try his fang and tooth, sweet sirs!
He will rend them, he is savage,
Thinking nothing but to ravage,
Nor with cudgel, fire, rope,
May ye control my misanthrope;
He would tear the moon in the sky
And fly at Heaven, could he fly.
And for his ravening without cease
I have had of him no peace;
Only once I bared the knife
To quit my devil of his life,
But listen, how I heard him say,
"Think you I shall die today?
Since your mother cursed and died,
I am keeping at your side,
We are firmly knit together,
Two ends tugging at one tether,
And you shall see when I shall die
That you are mortal even as I."
Bring your stoutest-hearted curs
If ye would risk him, gentle sirs.

Countrymen, here's a noble frame,
Humphrey is my elephant's name.
When my father's back was bent
Under steep impediment,
Humphrey came to my possession,
With patient strength for all his passion.
Have ye a mountain to remove?
It is Humphrey's dearest love.
Pile his burden to the skies,
Loose a pestilence of flies,
Foot him in the quick morass
Where no laden beast can pass,
He will staunch his weariless back
And march unswerving on the track.
Have ye seen a back so wide,
So impenetrable hide?
Nor think ye by this Humphrey hill
Prince Hamlet bare his fardels ill?
Myself I like it not for us
To wear beneath an incubus,
I take offence, but in no rage
May I dispose my heritage;
Though in good time the vast and tough
Shall sink and totter fast enough.
So pile your population up,
They are a drop in Humphrey's cup;
Add all your curses to his pack
To make one straw for Humphrey's back.

If ye remark how poor I am,
Come, citizens, behold my lamb!
Have ye a lion, ounce, or scourge,
Or any beast of dainty gorge?
Agnus lays his tender youth
Between the very enemy's mouth.
And though he sniff his delicate meat
He may not bruise that flesh nor eat.
He may not rend him limb from limb
If Agnus do but bleat on him.
Fierce was my youth, but like a dream
I saw a temple and a stream,
And where I knelt and washed my sore,
This infant lamb stood on the shore,
He mounted with me from the river,
And still he cries, as brave as ever:
"Lay me down by the lion's side
To match my frailty with his pride.
Fain would I welter in my blood
To teach these lions true lionhood."
So daily Agnus would be slain
But daily is denied again,
And still the hungry lions range
While Agnus waits upon a change;
Only the coursing lions die
And in their deserts mortify.
So bring us lion, leopard, bear,
To try of Agnus without fear,
And ye less gentle than I am,
Come, be instructed of my Lamb.

Here lies a lady of beauty and high degree.
Of chills and fever she died, of fever and chills,
The delight of her husband, her aunt, an infant of
  three,
And of medicos marveling sweetly on her ills.

For either she burned, and her confident eyes would
  blaze,
And her fingers fly in a manner to puzzle their heads—
What was she making? Why, nothing; she sat in a
  maze
Of old scraps of laces, snipped into curious shreds—

Or this would pass, and the light of her fire decline
Till she lay discouraged and cold, like a thin stalk
  white and blown,
And would not open her eyes, to kisses, to wine;
The sixth of these states was her last; the cold settled
  down.

Sweet ladies, long may ye bloom, and toughly I hope
  ye may thole,
But was she not lucky? In flowers and lace and mourn-
  ing,
In love and great honor we bade God rest her soul
After six little spaces of chill, and six of burning.

Grim in my little black coat as the sleazy beetle,
And gone of hue,
Lonely, a man reputed for softening little,
Loving few—

Mournfully going where men assemble, unfriended,
  pushing
With laborious wares,
And glaring with little grey eyes at whom I am brush-
  ing,
Who would with theirs—

Full of my thoughts as I trudge here and trundle
  yonder,
Eyes on the ground
Tricked by bird-flights or women to no wonder
And no sound—

Yet privy to great dreams, and secret in vainglory,
And hot and proud,
And poor and bewildered, and longing to hear my
  own story
Rehearsed aloud—

How I have passed, involved in these chances and
  choices,
By certain trees
Whose tiny attent auricles receive the true voices
Of the wordless breeze—

And against me the council of spirits were not then
    darkened
Who thereby house,
As I set my boots to the path beneath them, and
    hearkened
To the talking boughs—

How one said, "This ambulant worm, he is strangely
    other
Than they suppose"—
But one, "He was sired by his father and dammed by
    his mother
And acknowledges those"—

And then: "Nay, nay—this man is a changeling and
    knows not—
This was a Prince
From a far great kingdom—and should return, but
    goes not—
Long years since"—

But like a King I was subject to a King's condition,
And I marched on,
Not testing at eavesdrop the glory of my suspicion,
And the talkers were gone—

And duly appeared I at the very clock-throb appointed
In the litten room,
Nor was hailed with that love that leaps to the Heir
    Anointed:
"Hush, hush, he is come!"

CONRAD IN TWILIGHT

Conrad, Conrad, aren't you old
To sit so late in your mouldy garden?
And I think Conrad knows it well,
Nursing his knees, too rheumy and cold
To warm the wraith of a Forest of Arden.

Neuralgia in the back of his neck,
His lungs filling with such miasma,
His feet dipping in leafage and muck:
Conrad! you've forgotten asthma.

Conrad's house has thick red walls,
The log on Conrad's hearth is blazing,
Slippers and pipe and tea are served,
Butter and toast are meant for pleasing!
Still Conrad's back is not uncurved
And here's an autumn on him, teasing.

Autumn days in our section
Are the most used-up thing on earth
(Or in the waters under the earth)
Having no more color nor predilection
Than cornstalks too wet for the fire,
A ribbon rotting on the byre,
A man's face as weathered as straw
By the summer's flare and winter's flaw.

Antichrist, playing his lissome flute and merry
As was his wont, debouched upon the plain;
Then came a swirl of dust, and Christ drew rein,
Brooding upon his frugal breviary.

Now which shall die, the roundel, rose, and hall,
Or else the tonsured beadsman's monkery?
For Christ and Antichrist arm cap-a-pie,
The prospect charms the soul of the lean jackal.

But Antichrist got down from the Barbary beast
And doffed his plume in courteous prostration;
Christ left his jennet's back in deprecation
And raised him, his own hand about the waist.

Then next they fingered chivalry's quaint page,
Of precedence discoursing by the letter.
The oratory of Antichrist was better,
He invested Christ with the elder lineage.

He set Christ on his own Mahomet's back
Where Christ sat fortressed up like Diomede;
The cynical hairy jennet was his steed,
Obtuse, and most indifferent to attack.

The lordings measured lances and stood still,
And each was loath to let the other's blood;
Originally they were one brotherhood;
There stood the white pavilion on the hill.

To the pavilion went then the hierarchs,
If they might truce their honorable dispute;
Firm was the Christian's chin and he was mute,
And Antichrist ejected scant remarks.

Antichrist tendered a spray of rosemary
To serve his brother for a buttonhole;
Then Christ about his adversary's poll
Wrapped a dry palm that grew on Calvary.

Christ wore a dusty cassock, and the knight
Did him the honors of his tiring-hall,
Whence Christ did not come forth too finical,
But his egregious beauty richly dight.

With feasting they concluded every day,
And when the other shaped his phrases thicker
Christ, introducing water in the liquor,
Made wine of more ethereal bouquet.

At wassail Antichrist would pitch the strain
For unison of all the retinue;
Christ beat the time, and hummed a stave or two,
But did not say the words, which were profane.

Perruquiers were privily presented,
Till, knowing his need extreme and his heart pure,
Christ let them dress him his thick chevelure,
And soon his beard was glozed and sweetly scented.

And so the Wolf said Brother to the Lamb,
The True Heir keeping with the poor Impostor,
The rubric and the holy paternoster
Were jangled strangely with the dithyramb.

It could not be. There was a patriarch,
A godly liege of old malignant brood,
Who could not fathom the new brotherhood
Between the children of the light and dark.

He sought the ear of Christ on these strange things,
But in the white pavilion when he stood,
And saw them favored and dressed like twins at food,
Profound and mad became his misgivings.

The voices, and their burdens, he must hear,
But equal between the pleasant Princes flew
Theology, the arts, the old customs and the new;
Hoarsely he ran and hissed in the wrong ear.

He was discomfited, but Christ much more.
Christ sheds unmannerly his devil's pelf,
Takes ashes from the hearth and smears himself,
Calls for his smock and jennet as before.

His trump recalls his own to right opinions,
With scourge they mortify their carnal selves,
With stone they whet the ax-heads on the helves
And seek the Prince Beelzebub and minions.

Christ and his myrmidons, Christ at the head,
Chanted of death and glory and no complaisance;
Antichrist and the armies of malfeasance
Made songs of innocence and no bloodshed.

The immortal Adversary shook his head:
If now they fought too long, then he would famish;
And if much blood was shed, why, he was squeamish:
"These Armageddons weary me much," he said.

Beautiful as the flying legend of some leopard
She had not yet chosen her great captain or prince
Depositary to her flesh, and our defense;
And a wandering beauty is a blade out of its scabbard.
You know how dangerous, gentlemen of threescore?
May you know it yet ten more.

Nor by process of veiling she grew the less fabulous.
Grey or blue veils, we were desperate to study
The invincible emanations of her white body,
And the winds at her ordered raiment were ominous.
Might she walk in the market, sit in the council of
    soldiers?
Only of the extreme elders.

But a rare chance was the girl's then, when the Invader
Trumpeted from the south, and rumbled from the
    north,
Beleaguered the city from four quarters of the earth,
Our soldiery too craven and sick to aid her—
Where were the arms could countervail this horde?
Her beauty was the sword.

She sat with the elders, and proved on their blear
    visage
How bright was the weapon unrusted in her keeping,
While he lay surfeiting on their harvest heaping,
Wasting the husbandry of their rarest vintage—
And dreaming of the broad-breasted dames for con-
    cubine?
These floated on his wine.

He was lapped with bay-leaves, and grass and fumiter
    weed,
And from under the wine-film encountered his mortal
    vision,
For even within his tent she accomplished his derision;
She loosed one veil and another, standing unafraid;
And he perished. Nor brushed her with even so much
    as a daisy?
She found his destruction easy.

The heathen are all perished. The victory was fur-
    nished,
We smote them hiding in our vineyards, barns, an-
    nexes,
And now their white bones clutter the holes of foxes,
And the chieftain's head, with grinning sockets, and
    varnished—
Is it hung on the sky with a hideous epitaphy?
No, the woman keeps the trophy.

May God send unto our virtuous lady her prince.
It is stated she went reluctant to that orgy,
Yet a madness fevers our young men, and not the
    clergy
Nor the elders have turned them unto modesty since.
Inflamed by the thought of her naked beauty with
    desire?
Yes, and chilled with fear and despair.

Twirling your blue skirts, travelling the sward
Under the towers of your seminary,
Go listen to your teachers old and contrary
Without believing a word.

Tie the white fillets then about your hair
And think no more of what will come to pass
Than bluebirds that go walking on the grass
And chattering on the air.

Practise your beauty, blue girls, before it fail;
And I will cry with my loud lips and publish
Beauty which all our power shall never establish,
It is so frail.

For I could tell you a story which is true;
I know a lady with a terrible tongue,
Blear eyes fallen from blue,
All her perfections tarnished—yet it is not long
Since she was lovelier than any of you.

Procne, Philomela, and Itylus,
Your names are liquid, your improbable tale
Is recited in the classic numbers of the nightingale.
Ah, but our numbers are not felicitous,
It goes not liquidly for us.

Perched on a Roman ilex, and duly apostrophized,
The nightingale descanted unto Ovid;
She has even appeared to the Teutons, the swilled and
    gravid;
At Fontainebleau it may be the bird was gallicized;
Never was she baptized.

To England came Philomela with her pain,
Fleeing the hawk her husband; querulous ghost,
She wanders when he sits heavy on his roost,
Utters herself in the original again,
The untranslatable refrain.

Not to these shores she came! this other Thrace,
Environ barbarous to the royal Attic;
How could her delicate dirge run democratic,
Delivered in a cloudless boundless public place
To an inordinate race?

I pernoctated with the Oxford students once,
And in the quadrangles, in the cloisters, on the Cher,
Precociously knocked at antique doors ajar,
Fatuously touched the hems of the hierophants,
Sick of my dissonance.

I went out to Bagley Wood, I climbed the hill;
Even the moon had slanted off in a twinkling,
I heard the sepulchral owl and a few bells tinkling,
There was no more villainous day to unfulfil,
The diuturnity was still.

Up from the darkest wood where Philomela sat,
Her fairy numbers issued. What then ailed me?
My ears are called capacious but they failed me,
Her classics registered a little flat!
I rose, and venomously spat.

Philomela, Philomela, lover of song,
I am in despair if we may make us worthy,
A bantering breed sophistical and swarthy;
Unto more beautiful, persistently more young,
Thy fabulous provinces belong.

OLD MAN PLAYING WITH CHILDREN

A discreet householder exclaims on the grandsire
In warpaint and feathers, with fierce grandsons and
    axes
Dancing round a backyard fire of boxes:
"Watch grandfather, he'll set the house on fire."

But I will unriddle for you the thought of his mind,
An old one you cannot open with conversation.
What animates the thin legs in risky motion?
Mixes the snow on the head with snow on the wind?

"Grandson, grandsire. We are equally boy and boy.
Do not offer your reclining-chair and slippers
With tedious old women talking in wrappers.
This life is not good but in danger and in joy.

"It is you the elder to these and younger to me
Who are penned as slaves by properties and causes
And never walk from your insupportable houses
And shamefully, when boys shout, go in and flee.

"May God forgive me, I know your middling ways,
Having taken care and performed ignominies un-
    reckoned
Between the first brief childhood and the brief second,
But I will be more honorable in these days."

CAPTAIN CARPENTER

Captain Carpenter rose up in his prime
Put on his pistols and went riding out
But had got wellnigh nowhere at that time
Till he fell in with ladies in a rout.

It was a pretty lady and all her train
That played with him so sweetly but before
An hour she'd taken a sword with all her main
And twined him of his nose for evermore.

Captain Carpenter mounted up one day
And rode straightway into a stranger rogue
That looked unchristian but be that as may
The Captain did not wait upon prologue.

But drew upon him out of his great heart
The other swung against him with a club
And cracked his two legs at the shinny part
And let him roll and stick like any tub.

Captain Carpenter rode many a time
From male and female took he sundry harms
He met the wife of Satan crying "I'm
The she-wolf bids you shall bear no more arms."

Their strokes and counters whistled in the wind
I wish he had delivered half his blows
But where she should have made off like a hind
The bitch bit off his arms at the elbows.

And Captain Carpenter parted with his ears
To a black devil that used him in this wise
O Jesus ere his threescore and ten years
Another had plucked out his sweet blue eyes.

Captain Carpenter got up on his roan
And sallied from the gate in hell's despite
I heard him asking in the grimmest tone
If any enemy yet there was to fight?

"To any adversary it is fame
If he risk to be wounded by my tongue
Or burnt in two beneath my red heart's flame
Such are the perils he is cast among.

"But if he can he has a pretty choice
From an anatomy with little to lose
Whether he cut my tongue and take my voice
Or whether it be my round red heart he choose."

It was the neatest knave that ever was seen
Stepping in perfume from his lady's bower
Who at this word put in his merry mien
And fell on Captain Carpenter like a tower.

I would not knock old fellows in the dust
But there lay Captain Carpenter on his back
His weapons were the old heart in his bust
And a blade shook between rotten teeth alack.

The rogue in scarlet and grey soon knew his mind
He wished to get his trophy and depart
With gentle apology and touch refined
He pierced him and produced the Captain's heart.

God's mercy rest on Captain Carpenter now
I thought him Sirs an honest gentleman
Citizen husband soldier and scholar enow
Let jangling kites eat of him if they can.

But God's deep curses follow after those
That shore him of his goodly nose and ears
His legs and strong arms at the two elbows
And eyes that had not watered seventy years.

The curse of hell upon the sleek upstart
That got the Captain finally on his back
And took the red red vitals of his heart
And made the kites to whet their beaks clack clack.

As an intruder I trudged with careful innocence
To mask in decency a meddlesome stare,
Passing the old house often on its eminence,
Exhaling my foreign weed on its weighted air.

Here age seemed newly imaged for the historian
After his monstrous chateaux on the Loire,
A beauty not for depicting by old vulgarian
Reiterations which gentle readers abhor.

Each time of seeing I absorbed some other feature
Of a house whose annals in no wise could be brief
Nor ignoble; for it expired as sweetly as Nature,
With her tinge of oxidation on autumn leaf.

It was a Southern manor. One need hardly imagine
Towers, white monoliths, or even ivied walls;
But sufficient state if its peacock *was* a pigeon;
Where no courts kept, but grave rites and funerals.

Indeed, not distant, possibly not external
To the property, were tombstones, where the cata-
    falque
Had carried their dead; and projected a note too
    charnel
But for the honeysuckle on its intricate stalk.

Stability was the character of its rectangle
Whose line was seen in part and guessed in part
Through trees. Decay was the tone of old brick and
    shingle.
Green blinds dragging frightened the watchful heart

To assert, "Your mansion, long and richly inhabited,
Its exits and entrances suiting the children of men,
Will not for ever be thus, O man, exhibited,
And one had best hurry to enter it if one can."

And at last, with my happier angel's own temerity,
Did I clang their brazen knocker against the door,
To beg their dole of a look, in simple charity,
Or crumbs of legend dropping from their great store.

But it came to nothing—and may so gross denial
Which has been deplored with a beating of the breast
Never shorten the tired historian, loyal
To acknowledge defeat and discover a new quest—

The old mistress was ill, and sent my dismissal
By one even more wrappered and lean and dark
Than that wrapped concierge and imperturbable vassal
Who bids you begone from her master's Gothic park.

Emphatically, the old house crumbled; the ruins
Would litter, as already the leaves, this petted sward;
And no annalist went in to the lords or the peons;
The antiquary would finger the bits of shard.

But on retreating I saw myself in the token,
How loving from my foreign weed the feather curled
On the languid air; and I went with courage shaken
To dip, alas, into some unseemlier world.

PIAZZA PIECE

—I am a gentleman in a dustcoat trying
To make you hear. Your ears are soft and small
And listen to an old man not at all,
They want the young men's whispering and sighing.
But see the roses on your trellis dying
And hear the spectral singing of the moon;
For I must have my lovely lady soon,
I am a gentleman in a dustcoat trying.

—I am a lady young in beauty waiting
Until my truelove comes, and then we kiss.
But what grey man among the vines is this
Whose words are dry and faint as in a dream?
Back from my trellis, Sir, before I scream!
I am a lady young in beauty waiting.

JANE SNEED BEGAN IT: My poor John, alas,
Ten years ago, pretty it was in a ring
To run as boys and girls do in the grass—
At that time leap and hollo and skip and sing
Came easily to pass.

And precious little innocents were we.
Said a boy, "Now shall we let her be the fox?"
Or a girl, "Now which of you will climb the tree?"
We were quick-foot the deer, strong-back the ox,
We were the busy bee.

JOHN BLACK SAID: I'll interpret what you mean.
Our infant selves played happily with our others,
The cunning me and mine came not between
Which like a sword is, O sweethearts and brothers
Numberless, who have seen.

JANE SNEED: I till you what I used to do.
For joy I used to run by river or wood
To see with what speed all came trooping too;
Those days I could not quit you if I would,
Nor yet quit me could you.

JOHN BLACK RETURNED: But now, Jane, it appears
We are sly travelers, keeping good lookout
Against the face whose ravage cries for tears;
Old friends, ill met; and supposing I call out,
"Draw nigh, friend of these years"—

Before he think of any reason wny,
The features of that man resolve and burn
For one long look—but then the flame must die.
The cold hearts in us mortally return,
We must not fructify.

JANE SNEED SAID BITTERLY: Why, John, you are right.
We were spendthrifts of joy when we were young,
But we became usurious, and in fright
Conceived that such a waste of days was wrong
For marchers unto night.

JOHN BLACK SAID: Yes, exactly, that was when
It happened. For Time involved us: in his toils
We learned to fear. And every day since then
We are mortals teasing for immortal spoils,
Desperate women and men.

JANE SNEED CONSENTED: It was nothing but this.
Love suffereth long, is kind—but not in fear.
For boys run banded, and simple sweethearts kiss,
Till in one day the dream of Death appear—
Then metamorphosis.

JOHN BLACK SAID: To explain mistrust and wars,
Theogony has a black witch with hell's broth;
Or a preposterous marriage of fleshless stars;
Or the Fiend's own naked person; or God wroth
Fingering his red scars.

And philosophy, an art of equal worth,
Tells of a flaw in the firmament—spots in the sun—
A Third Day's error when the upheaving earth
Was young and prime—a Fate reposed upon
The born before their birth.

JANE SNEED WITH GRIM LIPS MOCKED HIM: Who can
   tell—
Not I, not you—about those mysteries!
Something, John Black, came flapping out of hell
And wrought between us, and the chasm is
Digged, and it digged it well.

JOHN BLACK IN DEPRECATION SAID: Be sure
That love has suffered a most fatal eclipse;
All brotherhoods, filialities insecure;
Lovers compounding honey on their lips
With deep doubts to endure.

JANE SNEED SIGHED SLOWLY: I suppose it stands
Just so. Yet I can picture happiness—
Perhaps there wander lovers in some lands
Who when Night comes, when it is fathomless,
Consort their little hands;

And well, John Black the darkened lovers may,
The hands hold much of heat in little storage,
The eyes are almost torches good as day,
And one flame to the other flame cries Courage,
When heart to heart slide they;

So they keep unafraid the whole night through,
Till the sun of a sudden glowing through the bushes
They wake and laugh, their eyes again are blue,
And listen! are those not the doves, the thrushes?
Look there! the golden dew.

JOHN BLACK'S THE LAST SAY THEN: O innocent dove,
This is a dream. We lovers mournfully
Exchange our bleak despairs. We are one part love
And nine parts bitter thought. As well might be
Beneath ground as above.

VISION BY SWEETWATER

Go and ask Robin to bring the girls over
To Sweetwater, said my Aunt; and that was why
It was like a dream of ladies sweeping by
The willows, clouds, deep meadowgrass, and the river.

Robin's sisters and my Aunt's lily daughter
Laughed and talked, and tinkled light as wrens
If there were a little colony all hens
To go walking by the steep turn of Sweetwater.

Let them alone, dear Aunt, just for one minute
Till I go fishing in the dark of my mind:
Where have I seen before, against the wind,
These bright virgins, robed and bare of bonnet,

Flowing with music of their strange quick tongue
And adventuring with delicate paces by the stream,—
Myself a child, old suddenly at the scream
From one of the white throats which it hid among?

To a woman that I knew
Were eyes of an extravagant hue:
Viz., china blue.

Those I wear upon my head
Are sometimes green and sometimes red,
I said.

My mother's eyes are wet and blear,
My little sister's are not clear,
Poor silly dear.

It must be given to but few,
A pair of eyes so utter blue
And new;

Where does she keep them from this glare
Of the monstrous sun and the wind's flare
Without any wear;

And were they never in the night
Poisoned by artificial light
Much too bright;

And had the splendid beast no heart
That boiled with tears and baked with smart
The ocular part?

I'll have no business with those eyes,
They are not kind, they are not wise,
They are two great lies.

A woman shooting such blue flame
I apprehend will get some blame
On her good name.

PARTING, WITHOUT A SEQUEL

She has finished and sealed the letter
At last, which he so richly has deserved,
With characters venomous and hatefully curved,
And nothing could be better.

But even as she gave it
Saying to the blue-capped functioner of doom,
"Into his hands," she hoped the leering groom
Might somewhere lose and leave it.

Then all the blood
Forsook the face. She was too pale for tears,
Observing the ruin of her younger years.
She went and stood

Under her father's vaunting oak
Who kept his peace in wind and sun, and glistened
Stoical in the rain; to whom she listened
If he spoke.

And now the agitation of the rain
Rasped his sere leaves, and he talked low and gentle
Reproaching the wan daughter by the lintel;
Ceasing and beginning again.

Away went the messenger's bicycle,
His serpent's track went up the hill forever,
And all the time she stood there hot as fever
And cold as any icicle.

Beautifully Janet slept
Till it was deeply morning. She woke then
And thought about her dainty-feathered hen,
To see how it had kept.

One kiss she gave her mother.
Only a small one gave she to her daddy
Who would have kissed each curl of his shining baby;
No kiss at all for her brother.

"Old Chucky, old Chucky!" she cried,
Running across the world upon the grass
To Chucky's house, and listening. But alas,
Her Chucky had died.

It was a transmogrifying bee
Came droning down on Chucky's old bald head
And sat and put the poison. It scarcely bled,
But how exceedingly

And purply did the knot
Swell with the venom and communicate
Its rigor! Now the poor comb stood up straight
But Chucky did not.

So there was Janet
Kneeling on the wet grass, crying her brown hen
(Translated far beyond the daughters of men)
To rise and walk upon it.

And weeping fast as she had breath
Janet implored us, "Wake her from her sleep!"
And would not be instructed in how deep
Was the forgetful kingdom of death.

This morning, flew up the lane
A timid lady bird to our birdbath
And eyed her image dolefully as death;
This afternoon, knocked on our windowpane
To be let in from the rain.

And when I caught her eye
She looked aside, but at the clapping thunder
And sight of the whole world blazing up like tinder
Looked in on us again most miserably,
Indeed as if she would cry.

So I will go out into the park and say,
"Who has lost a delicate brown-eyed lady
In the West End section? Or has anybody
Injured some fine woman in some dark way
Last night, or yesterday?

"Let the owner come and claim possession,
No questions will be asked. But stroke her gently
With loving words, and she will evidently
Return to her full soft-haired white-breasted fashion
And her right home and her right passion."

TWO IN AUGUST

Two that could not have lived their single lives
As can some husbands and wives
Did something strange: they tensed their vocal cords
And attacked each other with silences and words
Like catapulted stones and arrowed knives.

Dawn was not yet; night is for loving or sleeping,
Sweet dreams or safekeeping;
Yet he of the wide brows that were used to laurel
And she, the famed for gentleness, must quarrel.
Furious both of them, and scared, and weeping.

How sleepers groan, twitch, wake to such a mood
Is not well understood,
Nor why two entities grown almost one
Should rend and murder trying to get undone,
With individual tigers in their blood.

She in terror fled from the marriage chamber
Circuiting the dark rooms like a string of amber
Round and round and back,
And would not light one lamp against the black,
And heard the clock that clanged: Remember,
    Remember.

And he must tread barefooted the dim lawn,
Soon he was up and gone;
High in the trees the night-mastered birds were crying
With fear upon their tongues, no singing nor flying
Which are their lovely attitudes by dawn.

Whether those bird-cries were of heaven or hell
There is no way to tell;
In the long ditch of darkness the man walked
Under the hackberry trees where the birds talked
With words too sad and strange to syllable.

The noise of water teased his literal ears
Which heard the distant drumming and thus scored:
Water is falling—it fell—therefore it roared.
However: That is more than water I hear!

He went still higher, and on the dizzy brink
His eyes confirmed with vision what he had heard:
This is but tumbling water. Again he demurred:
That was not only water flashing, I think.

But listen as he might, look fast or slow,
It was water, only water, tons of it
Dropping into the gorge, and every bit
Was water—the insipid chemical H_2O.

Its thunder smote him somewhat as the loud
Words of the god that rang around a man
Walking by the Mediterranean.
Its cloud of froth was whiter than the cloud

That clothed the goddess sliding down the air
Unto a mountain shepherd, white as she
That issued from the smoke refulgently.
The cloud was, but the goddess was not there.

Tremendous the sound was but there was no voice
That spoke to him. Furious the spectacle
But it spelled nothing, there was not any spell
Bidding him whether cower or rejoice.

What would he have it spell? He scarcely knew;
Only that water and nothing but water filled
His eyes and ears, nothing but water that spilled;
And if the smoke and rattle of water drew

From the deep thickets of his mind the train,
The fierce fauns and the timid tenants there,
That burst their bonds and rushed upon the air,
Why, he must turn and beat them down again.

So be it. And no unreasonable outcry
The pilgrim made; only a rueful grin
Spread over his lips until he drew them in;
He did not sit upon a rock and die.

There were many ways of dying; witness, if he
Commit himself to the water, and descend
Wrapped in the water, turn water at the end
And flow with a great water out to sea.

But there were many ways of living too,
And let his enemies gibe, but let them say
That he would throw this continent away
And seek another country,—as he would do.

SOMEWHERE IS SUCH A KINGDOM

The famous kingdom of the birds
Has a sweet tongue and liquid words,
The red-birds polish their notes
In their easy practised throats.
Smooth as orators are the thrushes
Of the airy city of the bushes,
And God reward the fierce cock wrens
Who have such suavity with their hens.

To me this has its worth
As I sit upon the earth
Lacking my winter and quiet hearth.
For I go up into a nook
With a mind burdened or a book,
And hear no strife nor quarreling
As the birds and their wives sing.

Or, so it has been today.
Yet I cannot therefore say
If the red-bird, wren, or thrush
Know when to speak and when to hush;
Though their manifest education
Be a right enunciation,
And their chief excellence
A verbal elegance.
I cannot say if the wind never blows,
Nor how it sometimes goes.

This I know, that if they wrangle,
Their words inevitably will jangle.
If they be hateful as men
They will be harsh as we have been.
When they go to pecking
You will soon hear shrieking,
And they who will have the law,
How those will jaw!
Girls that have unlawful dreams
Will waken full of their own screams,
And boys that get too arrant
Will have rows with a parent,—
And when friend falls out with friend
All songs must have quick end.

Have they not claws like knives?
Have not these gentlemen wives?

But when they croak and fleer and swear,
My dull heart I must take elsewhere;
For I will see if God has made
Otherwhere another shade
Where the men or beasts or birds
Exchange few words and pleasant words.
And dare I think it is absurd
If no such beast were, no such bird?

ANTIQUE HARVESTERS

(SCENE: *Of the Mississippi the bank sinister, and of the Ohio the bank sinister.*)

Tawny are the leaves turned but they still hold,
And it is harvest; what shall this land produce?
A meager hill of kernels, a runnel of juice;
Declension looks from our land, it is old.
Therefore let us assemble, dry, grey, spare,
And mild as yellow air.

"I hear the croak of a raven's funeral wing."
The young men would be joying in the song
Of passionate birds; their memories are not long.
What is it thus rehearsed in sable? "Nothing."
Trust not but the old endure, and shall be older
Than the scornful beholder.

We pluck the spindling ears and gather the corn.
One spot has special yield? "On this spot stood
Heroes and drenched it with their only blood."
And talk meets talk, as echoes from the horn
Of the hunter—echoes are the old men's arts,
Ample are the chambers of their hearts.

Here come the hunters, keepers of a rite;
The horn, the hounds, the lank mares coursing by
Straddled with archetypes of chivalry;
And the fox, lovely ritualist, in flight
Offering his unearthly ghost to quarry;
And the fields, themselves to harry.

Resume, harvesters. The treasure is full bronze
Which you will garner for the Lady, and the moon
Could tinge it no yellower than does this noon;
But grey will quench it shortly—the field, men, stones.
Pluck fast, dreamers; prove as you amble slowly
Not less than men, not wholly.

Bare the arm, dainty youths, bend the knees
Under bronze burdens. And by an autumn tone
As by a grey, as by a green, you will have known
Your famous Lady's image; for so have these;
And if one say that easily will your hands
More prosper in other lands,

Angry as wasp-music be your cry then:
"Forsake the Proud Lady, of the heart of fire,
The look of snow, to the praise of a dwindled choir,
Song of degenerate specters that were men?
The sons of the fathers shall keep her, worthy of
What these have done in love."

True, it is said of our Lady, she ageth.
But see, if you peep shrewdly, she hath not stooped;
Take no thought of her servitors that have drooped,
For we are nothing; and if one talk of death—
Why, the ribs of the earth subsist frail as a breath
If but God wearieth.

OUR TWO WORTHIES

All the here and all the there
Ring with the praises of the pair:
Jesus the Paraclete
And Saint Paul the Exegete.

Jesus proclaimed the truth.
Paul's missionary tooth
Shredded it fine, and made a paste,
No particle going to waste,
Kneaded it and caked it
And buttered it and baked it
(And indeed all but digested
While Jesus went to death and rested)
Into a marketable compound
Ready to lay on any wound,
Meet to prescribe to our distress
And feed unto our emptiness.

And this is how the Pure Idea
Became our perfect panacea,
Both external and internal
And supernal and infernal.

When the great captains die,
There is some faithful standing by
To whom the chieftain hands his sword.
Proud Paul received—a Word.

This was the man who, given his cause,
Gave constitution and by-laws,
Distinguished pedagogue
Who invaded the synagogue
And in a little while
Was proselyting the Gentile.

But what would there have been for Paul
If the Source had finished all?
He blessed the mighty Paraclete
For needing him, to miss defeat,
He couldn't have done anything
But for his Captain spiriting.

He knew that he was competent
For any sort of punishment,
With his irresistible urge
To bare his back unto the scourge,
Teasing his own neck
In prodigious shipwreck;
Hunger and rats and gaol
Were mere detail.

Paul was every inch of him
Valiant as the Seraphim,
And all he went among
Confessed his marvelous tongue,
And Satan fearing the man's spell
Embittered smote the gates of Hell.

So he finished his fight
And he too went from sight.

Then let no cantankerous schism
Corrupt this our catechism
But one and all let us repeat:
Who then is Jesus?
He is our Paraclete.
And Paul, out of Tarsus?
He is our Exegete.

Darkness was bad as weariness, till Grimes said,
"We've got to have a fire." But in that case
The match must sputter and the flame glare red
On nothing beautiful, and set no seal of grace
On any dead man's face.

And when the flames roared, when the sparks dartled
And quenched in the black sea that closed us round,
I looked at Grimes my dear comrade and startled
His look, blue-bright—and under it a wound
Which bled upon the ground.

"They got you? I have only lost a hat,
I would have sold the affair for three thin dimes,
But they have stuck your side. It must be looked at
And mended." "No, it's an old puncture," said Grimes,
"Which takes to bleeding sometimes."

"Why, Grimes, I never knew your mortal blood
Had wasted for my sake in scarlet streams,
And no word said. A curse on my manhood
If I knew anything! This is my luck which seems
Worse than my evillest dreams."

But when I would have comforted his white flesh
With ointment and flowing water, he said then,
"Get away. Go work on the corpses, if you wish,
Prop their heads up again, wrap their bones in,
They were good pious men.

"But as for me I have the devil's desire
For delicate tobacco in my pipe, and leisure
To stretch my toes in comfort by this fire.
Amuse yourself then some way, find some pleasure
Sleeping, or digging a treasure."

I could not find it. It was too melancholy
Sitting by Grimes my fortress who reared his head
Breached in the left wall, and subsiding slowly
To the defunctive posture of the stained dead
That now not even bled.

I, not to weep then, like a desperado
Kicked on the carcasses of our enemies
To heave them into the darkness; but my bravado
Quailed in the scorn of Grimes; for even these
Were fit for better courtesies.

Blue blazed the eyes of Grimes in the old manner—
The flames of eyes which jewel the head of youth
Were strange in the leathery phiz of the old cam-
    paigner—
Smoke and a dry word crackled from his mouth
Which a cold wind ferried south.

Cock-a-doodle-doo the brass-lined rooster says,
Brekekekex intones the fat Greek frog—
These fantasies do not terrify me as
The bow-wow-wow of dog.

I had a little doggie who used to sit and beg,
A pretty little creature with tears in his eyes
And anomalous hand extended on his leg;
Housebroken was my Huendchen, and so wise.

Booms the voice of a big dog like a bell.
But Fido sits at dusk on Madam's lap
And, bored beyond his tongue's poor skill to tell,
Rehearses his pink paradigm, To yap.

However. Up the lane the tender bull
Proceeds unto his kine; he yearns for them,
Whose eyes adore him and are beautiful;
Love speeds him and no treason nor mayhem.

But, on arriving at the gap in the fence,
Behold! again the ubiquitous hairy dog,
Like a numerous army rattling the battlements
With shout, though it is but his monologue,
With a lion's courage and a bee's virulence
Though he is but one dog.

Shrill is the fury of the proud red bull,
His knees quiver, and the honeysuckle vine
Expires with anguish as his voice, terrible,
Cries, "What do you want of my twenty lady kine?"

Now the air trembles to the sorrowing Moo
Of twenty blameless ladies of the mead
Fearing their lord's precarious set-to.
It is the sunset and the heavens bleed.

The hooves of the red bull slither the claybank
And cut the green tendrils of the vine; his horn
Slices the young birch unto splinter and shank
But lunging leaves the bitch's boy untorn.

Across the red sky comes master, Hodge by name,
Upright, biped, tall-browed, and self-assured,
In his hand a cudgel, in his cold eye a flame:
"Have I beat my dog so sore and he is not cured?"

His stick and stone and curse rain on the brute
That pipped his bull of gentle pedigree
Till the leonine smarts with pain and disrepute
And the bovine weeps in the bosom of his family.

Old Hodge stays not his hand, but whips to kennel
The renegade. God's peace betide the souls
Of the pure in heart! But in the box that fennel
Grows round, are two red eyes that stare like coals.

MAN WITHOUT SENSE
OF DIRECTION

Tell this to ladies: how a hero man
Assail a thick and scandalous giant
Who casts true shadow in the sun,
And die, but play no truant.

This is more horrible: that the darling egg
Of the chosen people hatch a creature
Of noblest mind and powerful leg
Who cannot fathom nor perform his nature.

The larks' tongues are never stilled
Where the pale spread straw of sunlight lies.
Then what invidious gods have willed
Him to be seized so otherwise?

Birds of the field and beasts of the stable
Are swollen with rapture and make uncouth
Demonstration of joy, which is a babble
Offending the ear of the fervorless youth.

Love—is it the cause? the proud shamed spirit?
Love has slain some whom it possessed,
But his was requited beyond his merit
And won him in bridal the loveliest.

Yet scarcely he issues from the warm chamber,
Flushed with her passion, when cold as dead
Once more he walks where waves past number
Of sorrow buffet his curse-hung head.

Whether by street, or in field full of honey,
Attended by clouds of the creatures of air
Or shouldering the city's companioning many,
His doom is on him; and how can he care

For the shapes that would fiddle upon his senses,
Wings and faces and mists that move,
Words, sunlight, the blue air which rinses
The pure pale head which he must love?

And he writhes like an antique man of bronze
That is beaten by furies visible,
Yet he is punished not knowing his sins
And for his innocence walks in hell.

He flails his arms, he moves his lips:
"Rage have I none, cause, time, nor country—
Yet I have traveled land and ships
And knelt my seasons in the chantry."

So he stands muttering; and rushes
Back to the tender thing in his charge
With clamoring tongue and taste of ashes
And a small passion to feign large.

But let his cold lips be her omen,
She shall not kiss that harried one
To peace, as men are served by women
Who comfort them in darkness and in sun.

SURVEY OF LITERATURE

In all the good Greek of Plato
I lack my roastbeef and potato.

A better man was Aristotle,
Pulling steady on the bottle.

I dip my hat to Chaucer,
Swilling soup from his saucer,

And to Master Shakespeare
Who wrote big on small beer.

The abstemious Wordsworth
Subsisted on a curd's-worth,

But a slick one was Tennyson,
Putting gravy on his venison.

What these men had to eat and drink
Is what we say and what we think.

The influence of Milton
Came wry out of Stilton.

Sing a song for Percy Shelley,
Drowned in pale lemon jelly,

And for precious John Keats,
Dripping blood of pickled beets.

Then there was poor Willie Blake,
He foundered on sweet cake.

God have mercy on the sinner
Who must write with no dinner,

No gravy and no grub,
No pewter and no pub,

No belly and no bowels,
Only consonants and vowels.

Full of her long white arms and milky skin
He had a thousand times remembered sin.
Alone in the press of people traveled he,
Minding her jacinth, and myrrh, and ivory.

Mouth he remembered: the quaint orifice
From which came heat that flamed upon the kiss,
Till cold words came down spiral from the head.
Grey doves from the officious tower illsped.

Body: it was a white field ready for love,
On her body's field, with the gaunt tower above,
The lilies grew, beseeching him to take,
If he would pluck and wear them, bruise and break.

Eyes talking: Never mind the cruel words,
Embrace my flowers, but not embrace the swords.
But what they said, the doves came straightway flying
And unsaid: Honor, Honor, they came crying.

Importunate her doves. Too pure, too wise,
Clambering on his shoulder, saying, Arise,
Leave me now, and never let us meet,
Eternal distance now command thy feet.

Predicament indeed, which thus discovers
Honor among thieves, Honor between lovers.
O such a little word is Honor, they feel!
But the grey word is between them cold as steel.

At length I saw these lovers fully were come
Into their torture of equilibrium;
Dreadfully had forsworn each other, and yet
They were bound each to each, and they did not for-
    get.

And rigid as two painful stars, and twirled
About the clustered night their prison world,
They burned with fierce love always to come near,
But honor beat them back and kept them clear.

Ah, the strict lovers, they are ruined now!
I cried in anger. But with puddled brow
Devising for those gibbeted and brave
Came I descanting: Man, what would you have?

For spin your period out, and draw your breath,
A kinder saeculum begins with Death.
Would you ascend to Heaven and bodiless dwell?
Or take your bodies honorless to Hell?

In Heaven you have heard no marriage is,
No white flesh tinder to your lecheries,
Your male and female tissue sweetly shaped
Sublimed away, and furious blood escaped.

Great lovers lie in Hell, the stubborn ones
Infatuate of the flesh upon the bones;
Stuprate, they rend each other when they kiss,
The pieces kiss again, no end to this.

But still I watched them spinning, orbited nice.
Their flames were not more radiant than their ice.
I dug in the quiet earth and wrought the tomb
And made these lines to memorize their doom:—

Epitaph

Equilibrists lie here; stranger, tread light;
Close, but untouching in each other's sight;
Mouldered the lips and ashy the tall skull.
Let them lie perilous and beautiful.

PRELUDE TO AN EVENING

Do not enforce the tired wolf
Dragging his infected wound homeward
To sit tonight with the warm children
Naming the pretty kings of France.

The images of the invaded mind
Being as monsters in the dreams
Of your most brief enchanted headful,
Suppose a miracle of confusion:

That dreamed and undreamt become each other
And mix the night and day of your mind;
And it does not matter your twice crying
From mouth unbeautied against the pillow

To avert the gun of the swarthy soldier,
For cry, cock-crow, or the iron bell
Can crack the sleep-sense of outrage,
Annihilate phantoms who were nothing.

But now, by our perverse supposal,
There is a drift of fog on your mornings;
You in your peignoir, dainty at your orange-cup,
Feel poising round the sunny room

Invisible evil, deprived, and bold.
All day the clock will metronome
Your gallant fear; the needles clicking,
The heels detonating the stair's cavern.

Freshening the water in the blue bowls
For the buckberries with not all your love,
You shall be listening for the low wind,
The warning sibilance of pines.

You like a waning moon, and I accusing
Our too banded Eumenides,
You shall make Noes but wanderingly,
Smoothing the heads of the hungry children.

WHAT DUCKS REQUIRE

Ducks require no ship and sail
Bellied on the foamy skies,
Who scud north. Male and female
Make a slight nest to arise
Where they overtake the spring,
Which clogs with muddy going.

The zone unready. But the pond,
Eye of a bleak Cyclops visage, catches
Such glints of hyacinth and bland
As bloom in aquarelles of ditches
On a cold spring ground, a freak,
A weathering chance even in the wrack.

The half-householders for estate
Beam their floor with ribs of grass,
Disdain your mortises and slate
And Lar who invalided lies,
The marsh quakes dangerous, the port
Where wet and dry precisely start.

Furled, then, the quadrate wing
From the lewd eye and fowler's gun
Till in that wet sequestering,
Webtoed, the progeny is done,
Cold-hatched, the infant prodigy tries
To preen his feathers for the skies.

Prodigious in his wide degrees
Who where the winds and waters blow
On raveling banks of fissured seas
In reeds nestles, or will rise and go
Where Capricornus dips his hooves
In the blue chasm of no wharves.

With the fall of the first leaf that winds rend
She and the boughs trembled, and she would mourn
The wafer body as an own first born,
But with louder destruction sang the wind.

So must the others drop, there where they hung
Quaking and cold, and the blind land be filled
With dead, till one least and last wind unchild
Her of the sons of all her mothering.

No mother sorrow is but follows birth
And, beyond that, conception; hers was large,
And so immoderate love must be a scourge,
Needing the whole ecstasy of substant earth.

But no evil shall spot this, Margaret's page,
For her generations were of the head,
The eyes, the tender fingers, not the blood,
And the issue was all flowers and foliage.

Virgin, whose image bent to the small grass
I keep against this tide of wayfaring,
O hear the maiden pageant ever sing
Of that far away time of gentleness.

By dark severance the apparition head
Smiles from the air a capital on no
Column or a Platonic perhaps head
On a canvas sky depending from nothing;

Stirs up an old illusion of grandeur
By tickling the instinct of heads to be
Absolute and to try decapitation
And to play truant from the body bush;

But too happy and beautiful for those sorts
Of head (homekeeping heads are happiest)
Discovers maybe thirty unwidowed years
Of not dishonoring the faithful stem;

Is nameless and has authored for the evil
Historian headhunters neither book
Nor state and is therefore distinct from tart
Heads with crowns and guilty gallery heads;

So that the extravagant device of art
Unhousing by abstraction this once head
Was capital irony by a loving hand
That knew the no treason of a head like this;

Makes repentance in an unlovely head
For having vinegarly traduced the flesh
Till, the hurt flesh recusing, the hard egg
Is shrunken to its own deathlike surface;

And an image thus. The body bears the head
(So hardly one they terribly are two)
Feeds and obeys and unto please what end?
Not to the glory of tyrant head but to

The increase of body. Beauty is of body.
The flesh contouring shallowly on a head
Is a rock-garden needing body's love
And best bodiness to colorify

The big blue birds sitting and sea-shell flats
And caves, and on the iron acropolis
To spread the hyacinthine hair and rear
The olive garden for the nightingales.

ADDRESS TO THE SCHOLARS
OF NEW ENGLAND

(Harvard Phi Beta Kappa Poem, June 23, 1939)

When Sarah Pierrepont let her spirit rage
Her love and scorn refused the bauble earth
(Which took bloom even here, under the Bear)
And groped for the Essence sitting in himself,
Subtle, I think, for a girl's unseasoned rage.

The late and sudden extravagance of soul
By which they all were swollen exalted her
At seventeen years to Edwards' canopy,
A match pleasing to any Heaven, had not
The twelve mortal labors harassed her soul.

Thrifty and too proud were the sea-borne fathers
Who fetched the Pure Idea in a bound box
And fastened him in a steeple, to have his court
Shabby with an unkingly establishment
And Sabbath levees for the minion fathers.

The majesty of Heaven has a great house,
And even if the Indian kingdom or the fox
Ran barking mad in a wide forest place,
They had his threshold, and you had the dream
Of property in him by a steepled house.

If once the entail shall come on raffish sons,
Knife-wit scholar and merchant sharp in thumb,
With positive steel they'll pry into the steeple,
And blinking through the cracked ribs at the void
A judgment laughter rakes the cynic sons.

But like prevailing wind New England's honor
Carried, and teased small Southern boys in school,
Whose heads the temperate birds fleeing your winter
Construed for, but the stiff heroes abashed
With their frozen fingers and unearthly honor.

Scared by the holy megrims of those Pilgrims,
I thought the unhumbled and outcast and cold
Were the rich Heirs traveling incognito,
Bred too fine for the country's sweet produce
And but affecting that dog's life of pilgrims.

There used to be debate of soul and body,
The soul storming incontinent with shrew's tongue
Against what natural brilliance body had loved,
Even the green phases though deciduous
Of earth's zodiac homage to the body.

Plato, before Plotinus gentled him,
Spoke the soul's part, and though its vice is known
We're in his shadow still, and it appears
Your founders most of all the nations held
By his scandal-mongering, and established him.

Perfect was the witch foundering in water,
The blasphemer that spraddled in the stocks,
The woman branded with her sin, the whales
Of ocean taken with a psalmer's sword,
The British tea infusing the bay's water.

But they reared heads into the always clouds
And stooped to the event of war or bread,
The secular perforces and short speech
Being labors surlily done with the left hand,
The chief strength giddying with transcendent clouds.

The tangent Heavens mocked the fathers' strength,
And how the young sons know it, and study now
To take fresh conquest of the conquered earth,
But they're too strong for that, you've seen them whip
The laggard will to deeds of lunatic strength.

To incline the powerful living unto peace
With Heaven is easier now, with Earth is hard,
Yet a rare metaphysic makes them one,
A gentle Majesty, whose myrtle and rain
Enforce the fathers' gravestones unto peace.

I saw the youngling bachelors of Harvard
Lit like torches, and scrambling to disperse
Like aimless firebrands pitiful to slake,
And if there's passion enough for half their flame,
Your wisdom has done this, sages of Harvard.

ESSAYS

■

JOHN

CROWE

RANSOM

OLD AGE OF AN EAGLE [1]

ELF-TAUGHT, Thomas Hardy knew a good deal about English poetry when, in his fifties, he laid the fictions by and returned to his first love. He was an honest craftsman, attending meticulously to what we probably think of as the three dimensions of a poem. First the plot, or argument, a human representation struck off smartly, developed clearly and rounded off to a nicety. Then the meters, which this poet loved with a passion and managed with conscience and ingenuity. And finally, the poetic language, the flowering habit of a thing that is alive, displaying its grace generally and coming into intermittent focus in special configurations of leaf or blossom. I am indicating such a careful sense of a complicated job as perhaps only the neophyte will want to hold to in the act of poetic creation. It may be that he can afford to forget the several divisions of his labor only if and when they all will enter into the three-in-one of a single habitual and unconscious skill. There is often in Hardy's poems the visible quaint rightness of a workman going by the rules.

I mean to say that Hardy never acquired the absolute sureness of diction which may confidently be expected of a score or two of poets in our language. In his innocence, which was like that of a primitive poet, he appears not even to have had his mind on it. He makes mistakes especially (as our knowing critics must find) in his poetic vocabulary, using trite and stereotyped

[1] When Mr. Robert Richman was literary editor of the *New Republic* he appointed a number of regular contributors and seemed disposed to take more or less what they might furnish. The present brief paper is somewhat expanded over the one which appeared in that journal May 12, 1952.

words, or archaic words, so that he seems to be trying to be "literary"; though it would be hard to prove the imputation, to make it consist with his character. If we open his big book of *Collected Poems*—in my copy I am surprised to find that at some time I have counted them, to a total of 811 precisely—the chances are much better than even that we shall shrink from some of the locutions before the page is out. I am afraid the chances are much less that we shall be embarrassed at our shrinking. But we should not be so shrinking. I have had Hardy in mind when now and then I have proposed a standard for determining the strength of a poem which is different from that for the strength of a chain: A poem is as strong as its strongest link. But I dare say it is not quite true; my proposition is never accepted. The fact is that we are severe with our artists, and one rule which holds for most of us is this: That is simply a bad poem whose unfashionable or dated diction the plain reader spots at the first reading. The admirers of Hardy, both English and American, seem always too wary of committing themselves in the face of his objectors. I think I should fight the objectors, if I were spokesman for this poet. There is too much force in his representations—in his *Wessex Poems,* or *Time's Laughingstocks,* or *Satires of Circumstance,* or *Moments of Vision,* or the war poems, or even the late *Human Shows—Far Phantasies*—to have them set aside for finicky reasons. And there is too much greatness of heart.

His metrical formations are clean and fresh. Oftener than not, he forms the handsome stanza patterns out of ordinary iambic or iambic-anapaestic lines. But there is something special in the way he can make stanzas out of variations upon the "folk line," which nowadays we call dipodic line. Nothing else could have been so surely suited to certain of the country poems. And how to describe it? It goes back to the Anglo-Saxon meters; it persists against the romanic or syllabic meters which followed the Normans into England. It lingers in the rhythm of the oral ballads; then the dominant university fashions in the Renaissance just about swept it out of existence. But in the eighteenth century it comes back into print, in the recovered ballads, and in Mother Goose. Into print, and into vogue as a popular form for second-rate poets to adopt wholeheartedly, the first-rate poets sparingly, but more and more frequently as time goes on, right down into our own period. There are just two things to look for if we would hear the dipodic rhythm. The lines are symmetrical, or balanced in the middle, and so are their fractions. The original folk-line had eight beats with a break in the middle; but by division arose the four-beater, with its own break in the middle; and if the stanza wants it, there can be some playing—as often in Mother Goose—with the two-beaters. At this point division ends, and hence the term dipodic, meaning that the line has two beats at least, and if longer has a number of beats which is some power of two. The other feature is perhaps the crucial one. Often a four-beat or eight-beat line will drop its last beat and look unbalanced; but so strong is the dipodic expectation that we allow for the missing beat by a full musical pause. Thus the folk rhythm has an extra musical quality, not in the syllabic or university poetry at all. It is tuneful. Hardy would have known exactly how this rhythm was scored in the hymnbooks from which as a boy he had sung by note. In 1867, when he was still trying to market his early verse, he wrote "Neutral Tones" in the rhythm, and here is the first stanza:

We stood by a pond that winter day,
And the sun was white, as though chidden of God,
And a few leaves lay on the starving sod;
They had fallen from an ash, and were gray.

81

The stanza consists in three four-beaters followed by the climactic three-beater. Yet the poet is sufficiently versed in the university meters to know that not only must there not be more than two unstressed syllables between the beat-syllables, but that *fallen* may count as a single syllable, according to a usage established by the stately poets of the Renaissance. He is at pains also to put the comma exactly in the musical middle of the fourth line after *ash*, as if to oblige us to make the one-beat pause at the end.

A poem which stands not many poems away from this, yet was composed much later, and peopled with familiar characters from the Wessex novels, is "Friends Beyond." It illustrates many of the poet's qualities at once. The argument is a fantasy of Hardy's very own. He is in his fifties now, still hurt by the trauma he suffered in his twenties—which were the 1860's— when he went to London, and the faith in which he had been nurtured was blown up in his face by the evolutionists, and those new Biblical scholars who for certain essays were called the "Seven Against Christ." It was a bad hurt, but perhaps only accented what would have been anyway the melancholy set of his temperament. So in the poem the spirits of the old friends who now lie in Mellstock Churchyard are whispering to him about their "triumph" in the grave: they are delivered from "terrestrial stress," and "chill detraction," and even "fear of death." They speak to him both in unison and separately. Thus two of them in one of the stanzas:

W. D.—*"Ye mid burn the old bass-viol that I set such value by."*

SQUIRE.—*"You may hold the manse in fee,
You may wed my spouse, may let my children's memory of me die."*

And the poet observes:

> *Thus with very gods' composure, freed those*
> *crosses late and soon,*
> *Which in life the Trine allow*
> *(Why, none witteth), and ignoring all that haps*
> *beneath the moon,*
>
> *William Dewey, Tranter Reuben, Farmer Led-*
> *low late at plough,*
> *Robert's kin, and John's and Ned's,*
> *And the Squire, and Lady Susan, murmur mildly*
> *to me now.*

Among poets there is more dwelling on mortality than on immortality. And there is something sporting, and purifying, in this poet's resolute irony. But he was to become easier about it as he would grow older, and he was already old. He had a gentle nature, and his humble industry was prodigious; how should the knowledge of death corrupt him?

The stanza here is composed of two rhymed eight-beaters holding suspended between them a four-beater which is unrhymed. But its attachment looks forward: In the following stanza it will give its rhyme to the two eight-beaters, and there a new four-beater will arise to give rhyme to the next stanza, and so on by unbroken progression through the twelve stanzas of the poem. This rhyme-scheme is no more nor less than that of Dante's *terza rima*, a form exalted among university poets. We have attended a startling marriage between the high and the low.

One poem which bears the date 1866 appears in a book published in our century: it is the dialogue of two sisters, entitled "The Ruined Maid," one out of the great number of his genuinely original poems. We

might say that it was the utterance of a youthful
amateur sociologist, except that we must add immediately that he has a fierce folkish humor. This time the
poem is almost pure in its particular diction, and it
should be in the existing anthologies. Is it in one
somewhere? It would be if anthologists were not as
a class a little timid; they or their publishers. But it is
easier for the gentle reader to take now than it would
have been about a century ago. I will settle here for
four of its six stanzas.

"O 'Melia, my dear, this does everything crown!
Who could have supposed I should meet you in
    Town?
And whence such fair garments, such pros-
    peri-ty?"—
"O didn't you know I'd been ruined?" said she.

—"At home in the barton you said, 'thee' and
    'thou,'
And 'this oon,' and 'theas oon,' and 't'other,' but
    now
Your talking quite fits 'ee for high compa-ny!"—
"Some polish is gained with one's ruin," said she.

—"Your hands were like paws then, your face
    blue and bleak,
But now I'm bewitched by your delicate cheek,
And your little gloves fit as on any la-dy!"—
"We never do work when we're ruined," said she.

—"I wish I had feathers, a fine sweeping gown,
And a delicate face, and could strut about
    Town!"—
"My dear—a raw country girl, such as you be,
Cannot quite expect that. You ain't ruined," said
    she.

The ferocity of the young poet of 1866 was fully resumed when he started again on his interrupted career. I honor the constitutional vitality which kept him fierce, and I think I can understand his occasions. They came when he was reproached for his unbelief by the believers; or when he forgot that he no longer believed, and was indignant with his old God for the harsh dooms that overtook so many innocent creatures. But the old eagle did not grow gentle in haste; and, not fierce, no proper eagle. I am glad that he gentled, and that he did not come to it overnight. I suppose this happy dispensation visits any warrior if he lives in health long enough. Perhaps one simply grows into one's crowning intelligence.

I recall my excitement when I read in the *New Republic* at least two poems which Hardy wrote in the 1920's, never matched so far as I know by another octogenarian poet. It would have been Ridgely Torrence who chose them. One was "Haunting Fingers: a Phantasy in a museum of musical instruments." It is not in the folk rhythm as I hear it, but has a virtuosity in that two different kinds of stanza are employed systematically. Five separate times there are two stanzas spoken by the instruments in the one form, followed by a stanza of narrative in the other form. The poem begins:

> "*Are you awake,*
> *Comrades, this silent night?*
> *Well 'twere if all of our glossy gluey make*
> *Lay in the damp without, and fell to fragments*
> *quite!*"

> "*O viol, my friend,*
> *I watch, though Phosphor nears,*
> *And I fain would drowse away to the utter end*
> *This dumb dark stowage after my loud melodious*
> *years.*"

> *And they felt past handlers clutch them,*
> *Though none was in the room.*
> *Old players' dead fingers touch them,*
> *Shrunk in the tomb.*

And it ends:

> *"A holy calm,"*
> *Mourned a shawm's voice subdued,*
> *"Steeped my Cecilian rhythms when hymn and*
> *psalm*
> *Poured from devout souls met in Sabbath sanc-*
> *titude."*

> *"I faced the sock*
> *Nightly," twanged a sick lyre,*
> *"Over ranked lights! O charm of life in mock,*
> *O scenes that fed love, hope, wit, rapture, mirth,*
> *desire!"*

> *Thus they, till each past player*
> *Stroked thinner and more thin,*
> *And the morning sky grew grayer*
> *And day crawled in.*

Still later there was a wonderful day when I found another poem, in a British publication: "The Missed Train," in five short quatrains. The speaker recalls the time in his youth when, returning from a visit to his sweetheart, he had to put up in a hotel room at a wretched railway junction, but he dreamed all the night of "the unwitting cause / Of my lodgment." He concludes:

> *Thus onetime to me . . .*
> *Dim wastes of dead years bar away*
> *Then from now. But such happenings today*
> *Fall to lovers, may be!*

Years, years as shoaled seas,
Truly, stretch now between! Less and less
Shrink the visions then vast in me.—Yes,
Then in me: Now in these.

It is beautiful, and final. We feel that this is the only
way, in just these verses word for word as they stand,
for the old poet to conclude his very late poem.

THE American University works with both hands, and the right hand hardly knows what the left hand is doing. The right hand discharges its obvious duty, directing the strenuous and ever-enlarging courses in the sciences called "social" and "natural," getting the younger generations ready to enter the world of affairs. The left hand directs the "humanities," and that is something different. I do not know if many humanists would care to tell what they mean by the term intellectually, and if they should not, we may think the left hand is not so sure what itself is doing. But the humanists at the university can tell you at once what they mean by the term professionally. The humanities at the university are the studies of English and other literatures. Now American education is such a huge and sprawling affair that it is difficult to know where the central intelligence is located. But there is clearly effective in it somewhere a fixed intention to make large provision for literary studies at the highest level. It is not that a person has to go to the university in order to have the literary experience, but it will be bigger and richer if he has it as the university has it. And I have to tell of that as I know it. He will be made to learn about certain technical practices in this art, for one thing; but they are word-practices, this being the art which employs language, the commonest and most intimate medium possible, and he ought to be put at home with them. Then, and consequently, he will be able to ask and answer more intelligently the questions about its mysterious power; about how the experience of a literary object works in the mind of the experient, and what it does for him as a poor creature with strange and almost inarticulate needs.

This is the most self-conscious of ages. We seem specially devoted to the pursuit of truth by self-knowledge. Socrates might have delighted to live in it; and even younger persons who do live in it are likely to arrive at the university already fixed in the idea that they are entitled to know, really, how things affect them; which is according to the modern temper, and the Socratic. I am myself an academic; and I have noticed that the young are a little difficult, they are critical of the studies at which they are put to work. It makes the humanists who stand over them a little nervous. Many humanists that I know are given to worrying over their responsibility; they have to assign lessons in literature, of all subjects; they have to induce a degree of speculative fury in the discussions, and make it do work, and to set the modest goals, which must not be too modest, of literary understanding. But the chances are, as I believe, that good humanists just in the degree they feel ill-prepared to give the courses will actually offer them the more cheerfully, because they can go along with their students, put themselves into the attitude of inviting a fresh experience of literature, and have it in the flush of their speculative consciousness. The humanists whom I esteem never stop being learners.

Perhaps the last sentence brings me to my topic; I am not quite sure. It is to be presumed that the humanists at the University of Chicago, in the 1930's, had their painful indecisions as to how to direct the literary studies when their own speculations were not exactly coming through on schedule. They were academic humanists, and exposed to the hazard of the profession. But it appears that suddenly they made a clean sweep of their difficulties, they took the plunge (after the fashion of some too-disillusioned Existentialists) back into illusion again, they returned to authority; by appropriating a program of studies not their own, and waiving the hard questions. I am not as familiar as I should be with the everyday style of their meetings; I know they had some of the ablest students in the nation at Chicago, and not only kept them busy but won them utterly. It is clear that the humanists in charge dedicated to the program all their industry, and certainly now it must be said that they executed it faithfully, for they worked like beavers, or like scientists. But it seems to have been a rigid program, allowing little freedom for the discussions to develop something in their own context and out of their own fury. And since it was a program which had to be recovered from antiquity, it was antiquated. This inference is hard to escape even though it was the *Poetics* of Aristotle himself which the Chicago humanists adopted for their handbook.

From time to time they have written individually about their doctrine. And now some of the older papers are published along with new ones in *Critics and Criticism* (1952), edited with an introduction by R. S. Crane; a book which will serve as the official version of the intellectual activity of these humanists. It runs to some 300,000 words and contains twenty essays by six authors: R. S. Crane, W. R. Keast, Richard McKeon, Norman Maclean, Elder Olson, Bernard Weinberg. It would seem that Professor Crane initiated and led the movement. In the introduction he explains some of the background of their thinking. They observed that the program of literary studies ordinarily breaks down into four special disciplines: language, analysis of intellectual ideas, history, and criticism. Without formally abandoning the other three, which are always in order, they elected as their special interest to work at criticism, the most neglected of the four; that is why they are here. There is no indication of how it went with them before they embraced Aristotelianism. Perhaps Richard McKeon, in the department of philosophy, had something to do with that decision, or at least with the finish and intelligence of their Aristotelian scholarship. He is a leading Aristotelian in our time, and has breadth of mind as well as learning. In the writings here he seems less committed than his associates. In the essay, "The Philosophic Bases of Art and Criticism," the perspective is wide, and there is a relativism in his acceptance of different critical systems at face value. I should imagine that his influence in the group has been a broadening one, for I seem to recall some sectarian belligerence in their earlier writings which now has largely been edited out. Perhaps he has made for what urbanity there is in the tone of the polemical essays here. Sometimes the reader feels that a rather abusive tone is followed almost too quickly by a conciliatory one, as if according to plan. But it should be said that these critics conduct themselves with as much politeness as we are used to having in such controversies. We can sniff an exciting air as of something momentous when men of character and conviction debate the meaning of literature; perhaps a little show of plain passion is only what was to be expected.

(The rivalry of critical schools is in this respect no worse than that of religious sects. And it would anyhow be a set of *humanists* which would be listed as the school or the sect, according to my understanding. If humane letters do not perform the peculiar offices of religion, one reason would be that they do not do what Arnold said religion had done: "attach themselves to the fact, to the supposed fact." But they refer to the same order of reality, and they do it incessantly, though they may do it discreetly, and principally by way of implication or symbol. Their effect is pervasive enough, and it might conceivably be said that the effect of literature is comparable to that of religion, and in the same sense. These remarks are indeed parenthetical, but they do say that literature is taken seriously, and its apologists are likely to show fight.)

I can find no reservations in their commitment to the critical theory of the *Poetics*. They are pure Aristotelians, if we will allow for a little necessary supplementation of the handbook; but perhaps this suggests that we should call them neo-Aristotelians. The *neo* will cover those extensions of the rules which have to be made if we consider that Aristotle's treatise is occupied with laying down the laws for poetry at large—a thing he does much too easily—and then with examining at length the appropriate structure of Greek drama and more briefly that of Greek epic; but now the critics have to look into Shakespeare and modern drama and fiction, where Aristotle through no fault of his own was unacquainted, and into lyric poetry, where Aristotle's treatment is missing. The program has to work now; it has to work in Chicago, U.S.A. But they made the adaptations scrupulously, and did not exceed their authority so far as I can see. Reading the historical essays in their book, we have the conviction that there has not been a group of scholars in the whole intellectual history of the West who have possessed their Aristotle so firmly and used him so uncritically; at least in this particular field. Theirs has been a great piety, as even the most disapproving humanist must concede.

And there was a time when I, for example, like a good many young men I knew, could not endure to listen to disparagement of my philosopher. I knew the Nichomachean *Ethics*, and used it for years as a sort of Bible. But when I got seriously into the *Poetics*, my veneration was a little chilled. The work did not seem commensurate with my literary speculations; by that time I had at least read Kant and Croce. And now that my own age has witnessed a flood of importunate writings by spirited critics, I do not turn back and sound Aristotle upon certain of our stock preoccupations with literature without making the depressing discovery that he is unfamiliar with them; and, presently, that if I try to force from him some pronouncement by implication, the starch starts going out of the whole business; clearly this is not the way to proceed in it. We still have to search out the mysteries as they offer themselves, and from where we stand.

But it is quite worth our while if we need a workout, and for me at the moment it is a point of honor, that we should see what we can make of the *Poetics*. That was an extraordinary passion, we like to say, which Aristotle had for making a single systematic disposition of things which went together yet seemed to be tangled hopelessly. The enormous complex of language which was the literary object challenged him. Common language suggested that a poem after all was a single made object, a *poieton*. So he asked, What was the human purpose in making it? and how then is it put together? The two questions really make one question; the second is not worth asking till the first is asked and answered. The famous definition of the tragic play is in answer to both questions; according to Butcher it reads:

> Tragedy, then is an imitation of an action that is serious, complete, and of a certain magnitude; in language embellished with each kind of artistic ornament, the several kinds being found in separate parts of the play; in the form of action, not of narrative; through pity and fear exciting the proper purgation of these emotions.

It is very full, as exhaustive as a definition had better try to be. There are a fair number of balls here for the poet (or the critic) to keep in the air at the same time.

But still there are two omissions which have to be supplied from context. The crucial purgation (*katharsis*) of the painful pity and fear is the form which the pleasure takes; pleasure is always the purpose of art, and had as well be named in a treatise on one of the literary genres; it is named many times in the discussion which follows. The other omission is from the constructive part of the definition, but it is supplied immediately. Aristotle proceeds to name four major "parts" in the play which have to be maneuvered in proper relation to each other constantly as composition goes on: Plot, Character, Thought, and Diction. Nor does he delay to declare that Plot (*muthos*) is the main part, the "soul" of the play so to speak, while the other parts are subsidiary, working for the plot, and diminishing in comparative importance in the order in which they are named.

Almost any literary critic is aware that Aristotle was exacting in his demands upon the plot. He was expert in his sense of the plotting of the Greek plays. He talked about the playwright's "invention" in giving the novel turn to the stock actions which came from the familiar legends of the old Greek houses; about "recognition" scenes and "reversals" of fortune; about "probability" in the actions as a better rule than factuality; about complication and unraveling, and the tragic ending. The discussion of plot is the largest and most lucid block of writing in the *Poetics*, and perhaps insofar as the Greek plays are strange to modern students it is required reading for that particular course. But what carries over into the study of any drama (or for that matter of fictions and lyric poems) is something else: the tight organization he would force upon the various actions composing the single plot. Each action must be effect of the previous action and cause of the following one, by logical necessity. Of course the causal sequence is not one of merely mechanical actions, since the human agency is guaranteed every moment by character, thought, and diction. But as to the close economy of the system, Aristotle is a perfectionist. One wonders if this necessarily follows from the purpose of the play as given in the definition. It is Aristotle who likes his plotting tight, but what the spectator or reader is supposed to like is the kind of plotting which provokes the right emotional response. Who is to say that he may not actually be better served by a loose plotting? Perhaps *he* will say. Or if it is a matter of pleasure in general, which Aristotle often appeals to, even when he is officially limited to the pleasure of purgation, the spectator again may say, and now he may even have a certain distaste for what is most relished by Aristotle. It really does not seem too important; except that perhaps a dismal prescience may weigh upon us here, and cause us to think of those odious critics to come whose whole vocation will be in seeking the "well-made" play, or story.

We come to the subordinate parts of the play. The terminology is a little strange for us. Character is *ethos*, ethical character; the auditors of the play are good men, and the protagonist must be an even better one, the embodiment of a virtue which is almost but not quite perfect. *Ethos* is not equivalent to the Latin *dramatis persona*, and our own "character" does double duty for both; a character in the play may very well *have* character in the sense of habitual goodness. But I do not see here any sense of still a third kind of character: the Shakespearean, modern, passionately cherished, almost religious sense of the total individuality of a person who is rich in vivid yet contingent traits, even physical traits, that are not ethical at all. This kind of character engages an auditor's love, and that is more than his ethical approval. It also engages a critic's psychological powers, and more deeply than

95

ethos does. But on this point the reader of the *Poetics* must be admonished that Aristotle is dealing with a stern Greek kind of play. He must emphasize the "universal" in character as the plot-material for these ethical plays—though probably all plays are ethical, whatever else they may be—and he would object to the particularity or accidents of personality as something which history was better prepared to relate than drama.

Thought (*dianoia*) is likewise not quite what it might seem. The word means a thinking through, and names the power to articulate one's thought throughout a whole speech and over a variety of speeches; a virtue of large-scale discourse. The agents in the play must express their thought and feeling forcefully, not once but through a sustained effort; otherwise it will not be clear how they think they are affected by the other actions, nor why they perform their own actions.

Finally there is Diction (*lexis*), or the power to use language for the small-scale effects which are produced by the words themselves, and the grammatical phrases in which the words are put together. Every discourse has its own diction, but Greek plays are in the "poetic" diction, and that has to be accounted for. For me it is impossible to say that Aristotle has accounted for it. Poetic diction means two things to him. One is its metered language. Aristotle knows his meters, and in one place appears to be thoroughly enjoying himself as he substitutes other words for the given words in several lines to see how the sense would be altered, but refrains easily from altering the meters. The advantage he finds in metered language is that everybody likes rhythm. But some one may object, for this must occur to every one: Not so much as that; why not leave the play to its plot and wait for your rhythm another time, when you can listen to music? I cannot see that Aristotle has any important use for the meters in a play or epic; or that the Chicago people have use for them in Shakespeare or in lyric poems. Critics generally never offer enough of a theory about the meters so far as I know; there seems to have been a singular lapse of the critical imagination. But the other characteristic of poetic diction as Aristotle treats it is its fondness for unusual words and word-uses; or what we call its figurative language. Aristotle knows the kinds of words, and of figures, and gives examples with the utmost cheeriness, defending some of them from certain named critics who felt outraged by them. These tricks make the language striking and hold the auditor's attention, or they sweeten or ornament the language and delight him. But does that not mean, in either case, that they divert attention from the plot? I should think there is significance in Aristotle's remark that the poetic diction is best used "in the pauses of the action"; is this not equivalent to saying that it will interfere with the action when that is at its height? Shakespeare's rule seems rather opposite to this; in his plays the diction is least lively when there is transition from one action to another, but in the midst of action the whole power of his poetry is working. Somebody might conceivably argue that Shakespeare was pre-eminently a poet (in the sense of being a master of poetic language), though also a playwright, and used the play to provide him with plenty of poignant occasions for the poetry. But it does not seem advisable to put the plot and the poetry into rivalry, or bother as to which had the honor to come first in his intention. Both are there, and both engage with our emotions, though apparently not quite with the same ones. Aristotle does handsomely by the plot, and has nothing very impressive to say for the poetry.

I could not if I tried find anything more shocking to say of Aristotle than this. It is a good place to stop. What will his gentle reader in these times think of a

critic who prefers the plot to the poetry and mentions
the poetry only at the end as if it were a small gratuity
or bonus? Here, I believe, is the biggest issue sepa-
rating the ancient philosopher and the Chicago re-
storationists, on the one hand, from the modern critics
on the other. But there is a little more to be said about
it. At Chicago they are entirely aware of this issue;
they do not evade it. They have five hundred words
to say about it where Aristotle had ten, and say them
perspicuously in our own idiom, though in the substance about as we can imagine Aristotle saying them
if he could have addressed himself to the moderns.
The place where their argument is closest and clearest
is the latter part of Elder Olson's essay, "William
Empson, Contemporary Criticism, and Poetic Diction."
Olson, by the way, is their best man in a long hard
fight at close quarters. The critic who identifies poetry
with a special language is under obligation to read this
essay and see if his confidence is shaken. Olson under-
takes to show in detail that there is little of consequence left in the language of the play after we have
allowed for what it does by way of plain denotation
in getting the dramatic elements of the action before
us; that is to say, after we have used up the substantial
prose base upon which the fineries of diction are
mounted.

There is no sign of yielding on either side, and my
report seems to conclude with an implacable quarrel.
I am scarcely of Mr. Olson's side, yet I should not like
any better than another critic to have my bravery
impugned, and now and then have a foolish impulse
to take up Mr. Olson's gage and fight. Still, I cannot
but wonder if the critics of the future may not find a
quaintness in this feuding. For a year or so I have been
taking occasional notes on a possible critical program
which, though conciliatory, will doubtless prove bold
beyond my strength. It looks a little better to me at

the moment, now that I have seen Chicago critics, with a temperamental predilection for plot, being so zealous against poetry; and, vice versa, other critics, with a temperamental predilection for poetry, being so zealous against plot. Both are right about the thing they want, but as to the other thing they are narrow, exclusive, "monistic" (to use the hieratic epithet which the Chicago critics hurl against their enemies), or "monolithic" (the cultural epithet which various and other critics have hurled sometimes against theirs). I do not like to let the occasion slip. But my ideas are tentative, unproved, and till now, even in brief form, unwritten.

I suggest that we think of a poem as constructing and realizing not one poetic object, but three objects at once. Two are familiar to us, though a given critic is likely to think that one or the other is to be found in the poem, not both. The third object is one whose presence is unquestionable but vaguely disturbing to many critics, and which is not easy to understand. But it is necessary in advance to agree not to underestimate the capacity of the poem for embodying three large-scale objects. The same words will be used two or three times, it may be, in constructing the several objects, though perhaps there will be some words used for one only. The final objects, to be enjoyed fully, may have to be taken more or less in turn. But there will also be the grateful sense of the poem as a whole, whose marvelous economy is such that you can take it quite systematically in three different ways and find in it three different things. Let it be understood, finally, that the three objects do not constitute a Holy Trinity, nor even a Hegelian triad; it is nothing like that!

I hardly know which of two objects should come first, as having the primacy in the poet's interest. But let it be the most obvious one among the three: the logical construct; the big presentable object which

most gives its own shape and extension to the whole
poem; the object which best asserts its right in the
world of affairs, being the social and ethical one,
wholly rational and reputable and useful. Clearly this
first object is the plot. Sometimes we think we had
better call it the argument, as when it is a lyrical poem
and the sequence is not of actions; but with all respect
to the Aristotelians who for reasons of piety cannot
abandon the idea of action. The words of the poem
build up this object easily when used in their simple
denotative aspect. And surely an object of this kind is
good for the imagination to dwell upon; Aristotle will
supply the description, and the encomium; it needs no
apology.

The second object is harder to find, and perhaps
some persons cannot find it. It is the big formless one
which develops irresistibly, though hardly without
technical consciousness on the author's part, all the
time while the public or logical object is being
whipped into shape. It is a community of objects
rather than a single object; a little world of objects,
with new ones constantly entering it as chance allows.
On the technical side, there is an energy in the words
that makes them unwilling to stop with mere denotation, and a kind of lead given them by the poet
which calls the objects into being. And the objects
peopling the little world are natural, given, total, and
inviolable. If "imitation" is the method of getting the
materials for the poetic construction, the imitation
which finds such objects as these is freer than Aristotle
was prepared for, and the little world it sets up is a
small version of our natural world in its original
dignity, not the laborious world of affairs. Indeed, the
little world is the imitation of our ancient Paradise,
when we inhabited it in innocence.

And now, within the same poem, we can pass from
one world to another. The first world is the hustling

one we have to live in, and we want it to be handsome as possible. The second world is the one we think we remember to have come from, and we will not let it go.

There is but one big construct left in the poem, and it is entirely visible and audible: the metered one, within which all the words of the poem dutifully assume their places though they may be very busy at other things. The rhythm of the meters envelops the two other objects, like an atmosphere; it is a constraint and a blessing too. For it is sounding all the time; it is a low-grade music making an elemental, cosmic, and eternal object. Very diffidently I venture to construe it. I think the meters are an apt imitation of the Platonic Ideas, and in permeating our two other worlds permit us to have them *sub specie æternitatis*. For the worst thing about those two worlds is that the objects and arrangements we sense so exquisitely and cherish so deeply are doomed; they are mortal. That awareness is never withheld from us in the poem, but quite the contrary. Nor is there any human equivalent for them, really, in a world of Platonic Ideas. But still that world has the distinction of being the world of the immortals, and we like to sense it presiding over us.

So in the poem we have here or there, and in some confused sense all together, nearly every thing we can possibly desire. It is the best of all possible worlds. That is to say, it is erected upon our actual and Leibnitzian world as its base, and there is no other kind of world to which we can conceivably make our human adaptation without mutilating our nature. Of course it is not really possible, inasmuch as we have idealized it and improved it a little by our arts. But when we settle down into that grim realization, we are beyond the help of any poems at all.

MORE THAN GESTURE

RICHARD BLACKMUR'S choicest papers on poetry, coming clear down to 1951, are now in one book: *Language As Gesture* (Harcourt, Brace, 1953). That is an event. There has been in general circulation already a pretty firm conviction as to the quality of individual essays; but now the size of his achievement can be sensed, and a pattern can be made out for the whole. Whoever opens this book—we must assume that he can read it; we understand that this writer like his subject-matter invites the prepared reader but repels the unprepared—will be quickly aware that he has under his eyes a series of key-pieces on important modern poets. He will not have read half of them before he knows that he is being furnished with a consistently lucid exposition of an art in its most difficult period. And when he has read them all, when he has finished off with "Lord Tennyson's Scissors," the one where Blackmur at last puts all the poets in their right places—what then? I believe it will be his impression then that the book may as well be acknowledged at once as a classic; as the official classic, in exegesis of the poetry of an age.

That is how I think Blackmur's book will rate, and ought to rate. This critic has the gift for getting at once into any corner of a poem and out again, with brilliant creations from that mysterious world to show. More than any other critic, he has *copia*, in this case a well of bright half-technical talk, which never goes stale; he can keep talking, keep pointing, till the poem is overwhelmingly actual in the reader's consciousness, and there can be no doubt about its reception. How does he approach a poet's work to perform his "job of criticism"? For one thing, he seizes expertly on the most distinctive quality in the work, puts it in a taking figurative way, and performs with it like a metaphysical poet who keeps his metaphor going as long as he can before he breaks away. Blackmur's sub-title for dealing with Emily Dickinson is "Notes on Prejudice and Fact"; he writes his second paper on Yeats under the title, "Between Myth and Philosophy"; he writes one paper on "The Masks of Ezra Pound," and another for the same poet on "An Adjunct to the Muses' Diadem"; and he entitles his second paper on Eliot as "Unappeasable and Peregrine: Behavior and the *Four Quartets.*" Obviously his critical deliverances are themselves in the form of literature. But in the end, when he comes to the close work, he figures that the organization of a poem is very much what other modern critics suppose it to be. A powerful sensibility is recording in the poem, and the result might be a tropical wilderness of dense figurations, therefore humanly a waste, a nothing; but an equally powerful scheme of order is working there too, to shape and manage the riches of sense. The poem is conceived under the familiar figure of sensibility and intelligence acting in opposed parts and continually inter-acting; like parties in a drama, or a dance; like a musical counterpoint. Blackmur can isolate the interactions in every degree of magnitude. I do not know what is meant nowadays by a "new" critic, and I will not call him that; I will call him a close critic, or an intensive one, by all means a linguistic one. There is no poem for Blackmur which is not good to the last drop; that is, to the minutest verbal animation. But there is more: Blackmur understands another interaction, involving a third part in the poem. It is the meter, and the musical phrasing. Here the relation is between the prose rhythms of the language and the imposed meters, and that opposition is fruitful too. The resultant language has an access of authority which is almost miraculous. But it is easier to find it in action, under Blackmur's pointer, than in the present abstract statement. The great consequence of his book will be to advance enormously the technical reception of poetry.

And that is my tribute to the critic, paid at the start. I worked at the book faithfully, though I liked the job, to make sure that I had come by my tribute honestly. Now I will be at my ease. Which makes me no better than the boy who earned the money to buy the present for his host at the birthday party, but having delivered it at the door returned to quotidian behaviors. I will do a little quarreling now. Perhaps I can afford to raise some questions about his book, which it can afford to have raised about it, being so strong.

I want to know if the passion which Blackmur receives from the poem is engendered in the leger-demain of the poetic technique, and did not simply come over from the original human situation with the objects to which it has been attached all along. Is it born of humanism or aestheticism? Perhaps in the human situation it was a great passion but a despairing one, thinking it might be vain; whereas in the poem it is exhibited so firmly and with such a perfect propriety that it becomes confirmed, and confident; I do not know. Now Blackmur escapes from the jargon of technique as well as any man can who talks about it. But it is remarkable how technical all his studies are; the poems are examined along linguistic lines, pro-cedural lines, strategical lines; whatever may be the gravity of the content. There is no ideological em-phasis; the social or religious ideas are looked at shrewdly, but they are appraised for their function within the work; even though they may be ideas from which, at the very moment, out in the world of action, the issues of life and death are hung. In "The Later

Poetry of Yeats" there is a passage where sentence after sentence builds up this impression:

> He worked into his poetry the substance of Irish mythology and Irish politics and gave them a symbolism, and he developed his experiences with Theosophy and Rosicrucianism into a body of conventions adequate, for him, to animate the concrete poetry of the soul that he wishes to write. He did not do these things separately; the mythology, the politics, and the magic are conceived, through the personalities that reflected them, with an increasing unity of apprehension. Thus more than any poet of our time he has restored to poetry the actual emotions of race and religion and what we call abstract thought. Whether we follow him in any particular or not, the general poetic energy which he liberated is ours to use if we can.

When it comes to Eliot's poetry, he thinks the readers do not accept the religious ideas quite as did Eliot himself, but only as serving the imaginative structure of the poems; and as for the critics, or possibly it is for the readers too, "Our labor is to recapture the imaginative burden and to avoid the literal like death." The language in these passages is serious and eloquent; they do not have so much of that quirky verbal play which makes his mean style so individual. But the stakes are high; he is repudiating the ideas as ideas, and reckoning their usefulness for the poem. He speaks of the "intolerable disorder" of the times, and requires "intelligence" to supply the pattern which will order it at least in the poem. The poet Cummings is studied scornfully as a member of the "anti-culture group"; which always works by "a sentimental denial of the intelligence." A frequent term is "rational imagination," meaning the ordering imagination which controls sensibility; and about D. H. Lawrence he declares: "No objection will be offered to the view of life involved . . . only regret that it could not succeed"; could not succeed in Lawrence's poems; for not being formed by a rational imagination. He says of Hopkins and Emily Dickinson:

> If their poems sometimes confront the super-sensible—and they mostly do not—it is always on the plane of the rational imagination, never in the incomprehensible terms of the mystical act.

No reproach is lodged against the mystical act in itself; but it is not serviceable for the poem.

I will cite just one more text:

> Poetry does not flow from thin air but requires always either a literal faith, an imaginative faith, or, as in Shakespeare, a mind full of many provisional faiths.

The passage goes on to say that the religious standard is higher for serious art than for common life. I think that must be so. But would not the sentence have read well before it came to its official place if the subject "poetry" had not been there, but the subject "The good life"? It would have been pleasant that way; an affirmation with a cheery protestant clank. Probably it would have been subscribed to by the most dissident of all the dissenters in Christendom. But not by everybody. Perhaps by everybody who could read modern poetry.

It is a simple objection that I make, that I think there is to make, against Blackmur; with the reservation, of course, that I pick him up where he did not perhaps mean fully the inference which I draw from the aesthetic rule he has recited so many times. It is rather as if Blackmur had deceived himself in his analysis of language when he defined the language of poetry as "Language as Gesture"; that would seem to be looking at the surface of the thing. No faith, no passion of any kind, is originated in a poem; it is brought into the poem by the "imitating" of life (to use Aristotle's term); it is the fact which is the heart of the fiction. I have seen it said that the poem is a place where fact is turned loose, to see what it will do, in the laboratory of the scrupulous rational imagination. But I should doubt if there is much to this empiricistic rigor. Ordinarily, I imagine, the faith is brought into the poem a little bigger than natural, but not quite too big for the farthest reach of the believer; in order that it may be confirmed there. The experiment is slightly rigged. But the effect is nearly as good; and it is a very human sort of thing to try.

I conclude with another objection associated with this one. I have not quoted the passages where Blackmur on behalf of poetry is discomfited when intruders with a haggard look break into the poem, take hold of the intellectual ideas, the faith, the principle of order, and bear them away to use in their own affairs. He is a little ungenerous in the name of poetry. Though they abstracted something, they did not thieve; the poem is intact. Blackmur understands this very well, and perhaps his real point is that the marauders claim to have taken something from the poem which was not there at all. I cannot agree. At any rate they are punished by lacking all the other things which they did not try to take from the poem and which they did not know were there. What these things are, it is the burden of Blackmur's big book to disclose.

It is my understanding that other collections of Blackmur's superlative essays are to follow this one;[1] and presently, a book of those he has lately been writing about fiction. It has been my notion that

[1] *The Lion and The Honeycomb* was indeed published in 1955.

Blackmur as a good humanist was not content with the pure aesthetic or formal values he found created so abundantly within the organization of the poem; and finally felt obliged to talk directly about those ideas, morals, faiths, which enter into the conduct of life. They seemed to him to be explicit in fiction as they were not in poetry. For it is a commonplace to discuss the ideas of fiction substantively; so that critics of poetry are always urging critics of fiction not to forget that there are also the formal values, even in fiction. But I should venture to turn this round. Is it not possible for the critics of poetry to forget that there are substantive as well as formal values in the poem?

THE COMMUNITIES OF LETTERS

THE heavy hand of politics is upon us in these times. We are aware of a long crisis, and I think we are generally anxious to perform our decent parts. Like Milton's meager Shadow, Death, we can snuff where we sit, where we live, "the smell of mortal change on Earth." It is already at hand, for some states and institutions, customs and ideas. And some of us are asked to reply to the question: What is to be the social role of art? [1] So far as my own experience goes, many inquisitions by the dutiful mind seem to come always to the same answer: the role of art will be pretty much what it has generally been. Perhaps that is not quite an answer, for what role do I mean? I will make a resounding generalization, which I hope will seem like assured and familiar truth: Art is the freest and fullest and most sympathetic image of the human experience—none of the adjectives can be spared. And, for all we can see to the contrary, we need not go to much trouble to figure its conditions and occasions, for art has always managed to shift for itself.

Not long ago Richard Gibson, a young Negro writer, made a declaration of his independence as an artist, and repudiated the services of those "professional liberals" who would have taken him in charge, financed him, and had him writing about nothing but "the Problem"—the race problem in America. On what grounds should he refuse the role? Scarcely on the understanding that the problem did not exist, or needed no workers to get behind it. He had gone far

[1] This paper appeared in a forum on "The Social Role of Art and Philosophy" in *Confluence*, December, 1952.

enough in his own writing to obtain the feel of his art, and it did not restrict itself under such a commitment as that. He had studied the writers of the age to see what literature seemed to be objectively, and it was concerned with something else than social and political programs. Here are some of his words:

> Should the young man still believe in his talent as an artist, . . . it might be wise for him to remember that he lives in the age of Joyce, Proust, Mann, Gide, Kafka. . . . The young man might do well to impress upon himself the fact that he is a contemporary of Eliot, Valéry, Pound, Rilke, Auden. . . . And, regardless of what some might wish him to believe, he shares as much as any literate member of this civilization the traditions that produced these men.[2]

He said further:

> Perhaps it should modestly and most humbly be suggested to the still uncorrupted Negro youth with an itch to write that he become not another *Negro writer*, that he become instead a writer who happens also to be a Negro; not because he is ashamed of being a Negro, but because he is more ashamed of not being human, of not being himself rather than a stereotype.

Probably it is shocking to be told that the pressures which he had to resist came from his "liberal" counselors; but we know that story. Those liberals are in their duty, and so much in their duty that sometimes they are excessive in it. And if they do not succeed in enrolling the artists, it is to be hoped that at least they will secure their journalists, their publicists, who will be a great force for righteousness, and not without their kind of distinction. Here, however, we are ad-

[2] In "A No to Nothing," *Kenyon Review*, Spring 1951.

vised that the art of the young Negro writer must be his own individual achievement, and that the interests which are represented in it must be as wide as the human interest itself. This is well said. It makes us feel that Mr. Gibson has started on his career with a right perspective; it makes me feel that here is a text for a representation I would like to make about the free artist generally.

I

The artist claims his freedom. He cannot hire himself out. The consequence is that he must earn this freedom by going on his own in society. He is like a businessman, perhaps a small one, but at any rate he is like one who is sole owner of his business. And nothing is guaranteed to him. If a kind of writing has value for its author only, there is no market for it, and no career for him. That sort of failure we observe almost daily, and we cannot afford many tears for it, nor try to arrange artificial support for an impractical kind of production. Of course the artist's career is immensely difficult, and slow to get under way, and the likely young writer inspires such hopes that in a humane society he is apt to receive special attentions from public-spirited persons or philanthropic foundations. It will be considered that he must have his training though the cost may be quite beyond his means. Eventually, however, he is on his own, and it is healthy for him. If he can produce the works that are wanted from the artist, there is pretty sure to be a publisher for him, and a livelihood.

The economic system provides sufficiently for art, on the whole, in its haphazard way. Art remains in continual production, or very nearly, and the artist secures his livelihood and is a free man. On the other hand, the public is furnished with the art it requires.

The art comes out suited as is natural to the powers of the artists, and also suited to the tastes of the consumers.

But we prefer to think of those varieties of art which come from very great powers in the artist, and minister to virtuous and "social" tastes. We may safely do so. That is a high-grade business which is transacted between the artist and his public. The product is hand-made, so to speak, or "custom-built"—though these terms do not do it justice. The skills that go into this work are not paralleled in the rest of the business world, nor the relations which form between the artist and his customers. The customer admires his artist extravagantly, and is happy to think of himself, if not as sharing in the labor at least as sharing in the understanding of its use.

Duty and delight attend upon the reader's response to his author, duty made so delicious it is not felt as duty. The writer's lively image of the human experience will not fail to represent, for example, heroic and elemental behaviors, and generous and "social" behaviors, and in such a telling light that his reader enters into them gladly, though vicariously or symbolically. As M. Malraux puts it in his beautiful essay in Part I of this forum, the artist comes "to build man up again and to remind him, in a low voice, of his nobility." The role of the artist instantly acquires a social character, and indeed that is its classical character, which we know very well. It is an inviting theme, but perhaps we need not pursue it at the moment. The social effect of art, when the art is satirical, is destructive of evil, and cleansing, and that is salutary. When it is affirmative and the artist loves his representations, the effect is tonic. It fortifies the faith. And there can hardly be a doubt that in this sense the artist supplies experience which is confirmatory, and he is one of the powerful moral influences.

II

But there is "modern" art; particularly, there is modern literature. The classical conception of literature does not hold literally now; at any rate not for a great many of the most powerful writings which this age has produced.

Mr. Gibson has been smart in naming the writers of the period to whom he would advise the young writer to look for his standards. First there are five novelists: Joyce, Proust, Mann, Gide, Kafka. Presently come five poets: Eliot, Valéry, Pound, Rilke, Auden. It is a good list. I have no doubt that there is scarcely a reader who would accept it without some alterations, but that would be just as true of another list. And how formidable are these modern writers! When we run through the list and review our impressions of them, we feel that few periods in our tradition have produced a company of writers of such brilliant intensity, and we know that there has never been a company of writers so difficult. Their achievement is revolutionary.

Yet these writers, as we go down the list, will be felt to be as conservative in their social intention as their vision and their conscience permit them. They have witnessed the disintegration of the old order of society by cumulative forces such as the destructive analysis of religious and intellectual ideas once universally held, and the change in living habits under industrial production. Their writings are largely in protest, and they begin by abandoning the old tidy compositional schemes, and the old plodding logic of language, as if to say that these are clearly inadequate for holding society together, for otherwise society would not have crumbled. They cannot bear the implication that this compositional order might be the symbol of the great order, the world order, for certainly it has not been an effective symbol in that sense. It is as if for them there is no longer any point in that irreproachable housewifery by which the sentences and the paragraphs and all the premises used to be kept so clean and shining. The game is ruder now, and faster.

The modern writers on Mr. Gibson's list are artists of great imagination and immense energy and valor. But I have nothing specially fresh to say about them. Except perhaps this, that they have been entirely within the economic tradition whereby they have had a product to market which was ahead of the immediate acceptance of their readers a little—for they have "led" their readers—and yet not so far ahead but that they have won their readers, spectacularly. And this is one of the functions of the artist. He is not consciously and primly a teacher, but he can bring the contemporary mind to a new elevation of ideas and spirits, and the contemporary mind, some of it, is willing to be brought there.

III

After a revolution, all events look pale. But this one already almost begins to seem a thing of the past. I should not expect that the innovations of language and compositional design which it brought into literature would survive in their extreme or revolutionary form, but something of the sort will surely survive. When there comes another literary period with a great creative energy, it will have a character that was not in the one before the last.

Perhaps presently the stories and the poems will revert in part to an older and homelier image of the human experience, and an art of smaller scale; but with a difference. I find myself playing with a conjecture which would account for a good deal of the most satisfying literary art. But I have to overstate it a little. The role of literature, it might be said, is partly, and in recent times it seems often to be chiefly, to make public not the area of experience which is already public, where the focus of attention is on the constitution of the formal society and the obedience of its members to the code, but that area of experience which is most private, and never comes to public judgment. This seems to me another and very probable meaning of Mr. Gibson's "refusal." I am talking now about something in the literary experience which the critics of the past may sometimes have received only unconsciously, and at any rate never talked about.

There is a small paradox in the idea of an experience which literature allows to be both public and private at the same time. But a marvelous technical invention is at hand by which the artist can make it public and keep it private: the "literary fiction" of the creative artist. Sometimes at the front of a novel there appears a discreet disclaimer of this sort: "Any resemblance which may be discovered in this book to an actual person is fortuitous and unintended." And university students are carefully instructed not to confuse the "I" of a fiction (whether in prose or in verse) with the person of its author. It is important to be told that the fiction is *not* history, and all except the most uninstructed readers will read it by that comfortable principle. We have our own kind of private experience, and probably we know a kind or two toward which we feel that our own behavior inclines, decidedly, if the truth were known. But if such a privacy is revealed as a matter of course in literature, the anonymity protects us, as it protects the author. To both of us it allows an understanding that is without impediment.

The writer takes the private experience and converts it into a fiction. In that form it is fit to offer to his readers. He will feel that their response will be significant only if the experience is offered as a fiction, and might be something else, something guarded and quite disagreeable, if it had to be offered as an overt and attested behavior coming up for public judgment. If now the response is favorable, there comes into existence among the readers, clustered of course round the presiding genius of the author, a community of a sort which could scarcely have been contemplated in the formal organization of society, a community of letters based on a common sympathy. How much more tolerant, and more humane, is this community than the formal society! The stiff puritanical censors cannot obviate this for long, though they may exert all their force trying to maintain the single standard. And thinking of the antagonism of the puritan forces to literature, I am startled to discover that here is where I came in, a good many years ago, when I undertook the defense of letters in my little corner of the modern world, as did many another young man of that time. But I did not realize then altogether what I was defending.

The title at the top of this essay was meant to indicate that the communities are plural. The public of any important writer forms one, and for a long time it may have intense consciousness of its separateness; it is not identical with any other. It is one of those minority cultural groups which have their rights in a free society as surely as individuals do. (I do not foresee any particular breach in the rights of the minority groups in our society; and the sprawling democratic society must have its cultural variety.) But the group has no organization, and no revolutionary intentions. If in some rude sense, however, we add all the communities up, we will have, in theory at least, a total community having a peculiar role. It may be regarded as a secondary society branching off from the formal or primary society, and easing its requirements, compelling its members to approach to the sense of a common humanity. The bonds in this secondary society are unusually wide, for they bridge the national boundaries, and even the boundaries of the languages; and they should be wide, for sometimes it is not in the least the massed populations, but only a few choicer spirits here and there, who can respond to an order of fiction advanced either in its boldness or in its subtlety; and a community must have members. But the bonds may be close, too, because in our time they are partly the consequence of that intimacy which goes with a fellowship having a slight suspicion of the *sub rosa*. How could a gentle civilization do without this community? The oversensitive among us would be solitary and miserable, full of guilt and fears, in our dark privacy, if there were not the generous imagination of the artist to release us.

ON SHAKESPEARE'S LANGUAGE

Wᴡ HEN Wordsworth declared:

We must be free or die, who speak the tongue
That Shakespeare spake,

he was referring to the heritage of Shakespeare as an official *exemplum* to which the English national spirit, if it should ever flag, might look and renew itself.[1] We will affirm the sentiment. But I should like to look for a moment at the literary estate of Shakespeare as a property both larger and more specific than that. Let us regard Shakespeare as a fountain of language, from which was to flow and is yet to flow our peculiar English literature. More than any other writer, he laid down poetic strategies that suited the language, and one of his practices will be my present topic. It was good in his poetry, and it has determined the practice of other poets; it is surprisingly determining today, after the centuries of revolution in every department of life; and here, on a continent he never saw.

The specific usage which I have in mind as having been so fruitful is Shakespeare's way of compounding Latinical elements with his native English. I say his way of doing it; it is commonplace to bring Latinical words into English discourse, and was in Shakespeare's time; but not to do it in Shakespeare's way. He made it his frequent way only after he had come to maturity, but there are many instances of it. Thus Macbeth has Duncan's blood upon his hand and soliloquizes:

[1] This paper was read at the Conference on the Heritage of the English-Speaking Peoples and Their Responsibility, at Kenyon College, on October 5, 1946.

118

Will all great Neptune's ocean wash this blood
Clean from my hand? No, this my hand will rather
The multitudinous seas incarnadine,
Making the green one red.

We need not attribute much conscious Latinity to the first line; probably the public of Shakespeare's time had quite assimilated their Neptune, and indicated possession by the epithet they gave him; it is a folk locution rather than a literary one. So that, if we do not stop on this line, we may say that the four lines constitute a passage in native English, almost monosyllabic, broken by that Latinical explosion in the third line. The last line is specially primitive, having three strong accented words juxtaposed with some peril to the clear syntax; for we wonder, I think, whether to take *one* as going with *green* or with *red;* but a locution like *solid red* while explicit would be mildly Latinical, and it is apparently Shakespeare's idea to follow up the Latinical third line by about half a line of primitive language even with its natural disabilities.

The two big words do not represent Shakespeare's Latinity at its best but they are impressive enough. *Multitudinous* is *multitudo* plus *-ous*, the adjective suffix used in English to denote that the noun root it attaches to is Latin, and doubtless itself an adaptation of the Latin suffix *-osus*. (The native adjective is formed of an English noun plus a *-y* or *-ish* suffix; and many poets have liked to stud their verse with homely *-y* adjectives; Keats for example.) Multitudinous has something to do with many-ness, but we cannot tell whether it means here that the seas are many, or that the seas have so many waters. A fairly synonymous word would be *innumerable*, but that is too easy, and too well assimilated into the language already. Tennyson used it in the famous line,

> *And murmuring of innumerable bees,*

but he did it, we may suppose, for the purpose of his
sound-pattern. Its Latin meaning is explicit and brings
nothing strange into its English context. Keats had
tried for something bolder when he described the
colored windowpanes of Madeline's boudoir as

> *Innumerable of stains and splendid dyes;*

where the *of*-phrase is a kind of English for what we
used to call the Ablative of Specification; that is, Keats
tried to restore life to a commonplace Latinical word by
recovering an original Latin idiom. As for Macbeth's
speech, we wonder if there may not be some idiomatic
relation of *seas* to *multitudinous*. And *incarnadine* is
one of those words from the Latin by way of the
French, Latinical in the second degree. It is the French
name of a pigment, here used by Shakespeare—probably for the first time—as a verb meaning to color to
the shade of that pigment. But its proximity to *multitudinous* induces Latinity into our consciousness so
that we stop and reflect upon its Latin meaning: to
paint to the color of blood.

We can readily isolate from the later plays of
Shakespeare many passages of three, four, or five
lines each, having just about this architecture, and this
poetic quality. They show a condensation of Latinical
effect in a context of unusually pure English. And
the Latinical words will seem fresh, the test being that
we feel obliged to go back to the Latin to explore the
full sense of them.

Everybody understands now that Shakespeare knew
a good deal of Latin, and for example more than might
be supposed if one banked too heavily on Jonson's
reproach that he had "small Latin and less Greek." At
the free grammar school in Avon he must have got
just the right amount of Latin to conceive a great

fondness for it, and to have its resonance always after-ward going through his head, and never to give up the sense of it as a once-nearly-possessed language, there-fore still a foreign language, teasing him to utter it. Jonson had a great deal more of Latin, and—perhaps this was a consequence—got used to it; he never cared to import it consciously into his verse. I am talking speculatively and like an impressionable layman. The vocabulary of Shakespeare has been analysed for its Latin and other constituents by careful scholars; for instance by the late Oxford Professor of Poetry, George Gordon. But in general it is my understanding that the Shakespearean scholars have not speculated upon an issue that would seem very engaging: whether there are not some principles, or habits, which might govern Shakespeare's Latinity as a literary instrument.

It is still a fact, three and a half centuries from Shakespeare, that many words now thoroughly ac-credited as English are visibly from the Latin; we are conscious of them as of a minority of not quite assimi-lated words; they bring back our school-sense. And we reflect upon the two large historic accessions of Latin words into English. In the first one, that of the Norman period, the words introduced were French in their immediate identities, but Latin ultimately; the transmission was doubtless as much by oral means as by literature. It is customary to say that this stock of new words had been thoroughly assimilated by the end of the fourteenth century, so that in Chaucer we have a single unified language, with no special con-sciousness when the words were from the Latin. The foreignness had gone from them. And we think of Chaucer as taking pains if necessary to use them easily, in order to help naturalize them if they were still not quite naturalized. That is the intention we mean some-times to attribute to him as a patriot.

The other large-scale importation was an incident

of the European Renaissance which came by way of
the universities in the sixteenth century. In no sense is
Renaissance or Rebirth the right name for the general
movement more than it is linguistically. The new ideas
that filled the undernourished European consciousness
were old ideas recovered, classical ideas; but reborn
with their original bodies, the classical words. Or they
are new ideas developing from the classical ideas and
finding classical words to suit. But we recall what had
happened to the invading words after the Norman
conquest. Were the Renaissance invaders likewise to
be assimilated into English and to lose their identity?

In answer I suggest that precisely this event was
imminent, that the Latinical words were disappearing
as such in the literature that was being written, but
that Shakespeare's example more than any other one
thing stopped the process. On this supposition, it was
Shakespeare who preserved the life of Latin as a foreign language still held tributary to the borrowings of
luxurious English writers. Without Shakespeare the
Latinical words would probably have been lost. They
would have been lost not by being dropped *out of* the
language but by being dropped *into* it—as countless
other foreign words have been lost within our capacious language and are now used over and over without any sense of their foreignness. Knowing as we do
that Shakespeare was of humble birth, did not attend
the university, and as an actor was like a man belong-
ing to a trade rather than to a gentle profession, we
often wonder where we are to look for the signs of
his social inferiority. Perhaps we will imagine that his
linguistic strategy was not the aristocratic one. Probably at one time, say just before Shakespeare's birth,
it was aristocratic to make a display of one's Latinity;
but toward the end of the century it was aristocratic,
on the contrary, to make no difference in one's speech
between the Latinical and the native elements, and the

display of an attainment of so common an order as Latinity rated as vulgar affectation. Was Shakespeare then a generation behind the best usage? But there is no profit for us here. His early plays are of nondescript Latinity, quite *à la mode;* and the special turn his Latinity began to take was a novel and literary move, not a social one.

The dying Hamlet says to Horatio:

If thou didst ever hold me in thy heart,
Absent thee from felicity a while,
And in this harsh world draw thy breath in pain
To tell my story.

It is one of Arnold's "touchstones" of poetry, indisputably a passage of first-rate quality. But its whole distinction is connected with the *absent thee* and the *felicity* of the second line. In Schlegel's first-rate German translation of the plays it comes as a shock to us to discover that both these Latinical items have disappeared, as inadmissible into that language. To an English linguistic sense such a passage does not seem to have been translated when we meet with it in Schlegel. Both the terms are weaker in their Latinical version than they would be in some good native version, but they are strong by their visible opposition to the native context. A German friend tells me that some German professor might conceivably say, *"Absentiren Sie sich"* to a favored pupil, and would be understood, but that the effect would be that of an academic joke. And we may construe Shakespeare's line somewhat in that sense, as the pleasantry of a young Hamlet fresh from the university even though uttered among his last words. But apparently Arnold, who is prepared to take the line quite independent of dramatic setting or linguistic context, did not hold this view of it; it is notorious that he declined any analysis of his touchstones. To him it is one of those locutions resounding incessantly in the memory, and so effective for the feelings that it will serve as a standard of what the noblest poetry must be like.

If Hamlet's speech will not go into German, where there is no Latinity, we can imagine the contrary case when effort is made to bring it into French. This is not a bi-lingual tongue either, but here it is the Latinity which is the staple and the commonplace. We may have had occasion to see what happens, if we consulted Gide's version of the play a few years ago. The Prince of Denmark's French is admirable, and if we say that Hamlet is not himself here, that his mind is suddenly less interesting, that his sea-change is a little ludicrous, it is only after explaining courteously that we happen to have heard his English. Now, we are often told that English is a superior language for poetry, and we must often have felt that this is said too absolutely for politeness, or truth for that matter. Yet it can be said safely that all Shakespeare's effects were possible in English, and that some of the happiest ones are evidently not possible in German or French.

When Lear finds his Fool beside him in the storm, his thought suddenly turns from his own sufferings to the condition of the poor. It is a kingly thought, and leads him to apostrophize privilege everywhere:

> *O, I have ta'en*
> *Too little thought of this. Take physic, pomp;*
> *Expose thyself to feel what wretches feel,*
> *That thou mayst shake the superflux to them*
> *And show the heavens more just.*

There is a slight flurry of Latinity in the *physic, pomp, expose.* But the key to the passage is *superflux,* a word that nobody had used till then, and, to tell the truth, a word that even this usage did not fix securely in the language. It would mean overflow; in Schlegel the German is *das Uberflüssige.* I judge that we all are reminded more or less consciously of Lazarus begging for the crumbs which fall—without being noticed because there is so much food—from the rich man's table. But I believe we should balk at speaking of them as an overflow. We are prepared to accept a bolder metaphor in the Latin than we can take in the English. Especially striking is the collocation of *shake* and *superflux*. The English is a little inhospitable to the stranger, does not make it easy for him. All we can think of really shaking to the poor in this connection would be the tablecloth holding the surplus crumbs; which would not exactly be flowing. The whole image receives more notice and not less from our having these literal questions about it.

Latinical practices as startling as this are unusual in the early plays, and they are also hard to find in the contemporary authors. I suppose nobody would expect to find them in Spenser. In the *Shepheardes Calender* there are passages in straight English talk and rude English meters, and there are other passages in good university language and syllabic meters, both effects quite nicely specialized. In *The Faerie Queene* this beginning has not been followed up. There is no end of innovations in words and the forms of words, but there is no particular consciousness of the Latin as calling for a different response from that of the English and there is a nearly fatal over-all smoothness in the tone; we do not sense any dramatic effect in the shift from one tone to the other. The proportion of Latinical words, if we may indulge in a very simple generalization, is too large for effectiveness.

In Marlowe the Shakespearean practice is sometimes almost hit upon. His

> *See, see where Christ's blood streams in the firmament!*

does not sufficiently develop the opposed contexts.

When Faustus exclaims on seeing Helen:

Was this the face that launched a thousand ships,
And burnt the topless towers of Ilium?

we have two bold metaphors about the force of
beauty, of which the second somehow does not strike
us as quite native English. Then we proceed to note
that *topless* is Virgilian, and too far-fetched and
"literary" to be a folk-metaphor; *Ilium* is Latinical for
Troy, as the place is known to English-speaking folk;
and of course syllabic pentameter rates in the sixteenth
century as Latinical, or at least Romanic, in comparison with English accentual meters, though it is
almost too common to touch us linguistically. And in
the scene before the Emperor there is a passage between Faustus and a heckling knight, in which a
magical trick is played upon the knight, who expostu-
lates:

Thou damned wretch and execrable dog,
Bred in the concave of some monstrous rock,
How darest thou thus abuse a gentleman?

The gentleman has not only a turn for abuse but a
pretty gift for the Latinities. And Faustus explains to
the Emperor in prose that he has only "worthily
requited this injurious knight." Briefly, we cannot tell
what linguistic development might have lain ahead of
Marlowe when he died before reaching the age of
thirty.

Perhaps I may be credited with looking rather
widely though sketchily round to find other evidences
of Shakespeare's kind of Latinity. Here I can only
say, and provisionally, that so far as I can see we have
to give Shakespeare the credit for the strategy in
question, and for its persistence in literature. If so, it
is a massive disposition within the language that he
accomplished, and not a small disposition. Shakespeare,

or something else, stopped the reduction of the Latinical words into common words, and held them in a
state of perpetual suspension and arrest. They are in
the language, but not quite of it. If our language were
a political sovereignty, we might say that the native
stock had welcomed the immigration of the well-
favored foreigners, whose mores, skills, and presences
were quite distinct, but had not naturalized them;
they became a sort of colony, by no means free of
the obligation to work like the regular citizens at
practical tasks, and indeed they were specially quali-
fied for expert or precision techniques; but expected
also to appear sometimes at the formal occasions of
society in costume.

This must be a unique status for so large an element
of a language to persist in. One consequence is to
give to the dictionary a special importance among
English-using peoples. It reinforces, and nowadays it
even replaces and shortcuts, the actual study of Latin.
For the students of literature, and perhaps even its
writers, one of the important services of the dictionary
is to show when an English word is of Latin origin,
and what the original Latin was and signified. Otherwise I do not know how they would understand
Shakespeare, Milton, many writers of the seventeenth
century, and occasionally a good modern. Of course
the study of Latin independently is better, but it is
increasingly a labor that may not be enforced. The
best educational argument for it, so far as I know,
would be that Latin is still a living language, and
lives in Shakespeare and Milton. It is a splendid argument to make to those who already know this by
experience, but a difficult one to offer to the unini-
tiated.

I turn to some other examples from the bi-lingual
Shakespeare; there is a wealth of them, and often they
are units of considerable length. Here is the Queen

telling Laertes about the death of his sister by drowning. Gertrude is a woman perhaps more foolish than vicious, but in the midst of her garrulousness and absurd sequence of pathetic fallacies there are irruptions of Latinity which are regal.

> Then, on the pendent boughs her coronet weeds
> Clambering to hang, an envious sliver broke;
> When down her weedy trophies and herself
> Fell in the weeping brook. Her clothes spread
>   wide,
> And mermaid-like a while they held her up:
> Which time she chanted snatches of old tunes,
> As one incapable of her own distress,
> Or like a creature native and indued
> Unto that element: but long it could not be
> Till that her garments, heavy with their drink,
> Pull'd the poor wretch from her melodious lay
> To muddy death.

We will observe the linguistic ambivalence in *pendent boughs* and *coronet weeds;* the rather sustained though crisp and energetic Latinity of *creature native and indued Unto that element;* and *melodious lay* contending with *muddy death,* a Latinical -*ous* adjective opposed to a folk or -*y* adjective.

We have looked twice at *Hamlet,* which is rich in this kind of Latinity. What will we make of the Sonnets? We can see how much the later ones advance in quality over the early ones, and we have been told that the later ones often closely anticipate the language, in particular, of *Hamlet.* One of the finest is No. 107:

> Not mine own fears, nor the prophetic soul
> Of the wide world dreaming on things to come,
> Can yet the lease of my true love control,
> Supposed as forfeit to a confined doom.

The mortal moon hath her eclipse endured,
And the sad augurs mock their own presage;
Incertainties now crown themselves assured,
And peace proclaims olives of endless age.

Now with the drops of this most balmy time
My love looks fresh and Death to me subscribes,
Since, spite of him, I'll live in this poor rime,
While he insults o'er dull and speechless tribes:

And thou in this shall find thy monument,
When tyrants' crests and tombs of brass are spent.

Latinity is frequent in this sonnet, and sometimes sharp. The beginning is vernacular. *Prophetic* (which is Greek if not Latin) is necessary to the sense, but its clang is nearly canceled by *soul* and by the fullness of the pretty image in the next line; this soul of the world is not Spiritus Mundi at all, only the hatefulness of all the gossips who see no future for this affair; but in the third line we have another technical word in *lease,* and, to conclude the quatrain, a shower of Latinity in *control, supposed, forfeit, confined.* The last of these words requires a knowledge of Latin if we are to understand that the doom is appointed to occupy a tract adjoining that of the love affair, so that at a certain point in the lover's course he is bound to step over. In the second quatrain *endured* is pure Latin likewise, meaning lasted out, or lived through; and each line has a Latinical qualification in *presage, assured,* or *proclaims,* though it would be commonplace except by virtue of its context. The third quatrain is the best from our present point of view. The vernacular at the beginning is brought up short in *subscribes;* and it makes a fresh start only to run into *insults.* Indeed, *subscribes* and *insults o'er* give the chief interest to this passage if we know our Latin. *Subscribes to me* is "writes himself under me" or leaves me on top; *insults* is "jumps up on," and puts Death back into his usual relation to his victims (the tribes who do not make poems); and to make the reversal explicit Shakespeare adds a redundant *o'er* to match the earlier *sub-*. The couplets of Shakespeare's sonnets are not usually exciting, though they are necessary to the logic as generalized conclusions. This one is distinguished a little by the crisp work of *tyrants' crests and tombs*. People would know each of these words, but at having the three of them together would feel that there was a certain preoccupation with their Latinity.

Here is a brilliant passage from *Antony and Cleopatra*, which is full of them. Talking with his man Eros, Antony plays with the whimsy that Cleopatra has so robbed him of his substance that he has lost visibility.

ANT. *Eros, thou yet behold'st me?*

EROS. *Ay, noble lord.*

ANT. *Sometime we see a cloud that's dragonish,*
 A vapor sometime like a bear or lion,
 A tower'd citadel, a pendent rock,
 A forked mountain, or blue promontory
 With trees upon 't, that nod unto the world
 And mock our eyes with air. Thou has seen these signs;
 They are black vesper's pageants.

EROS. *Ay, my lord.*

ANT. *That which is now a horse, even with a thought*
 The rack dislimns and makes it indistinct
 As water is in water.

The Latinical effects here are subtle, but still entirely

distinct. The context consists of many primitive folk-items: dragon, tower, rock, forked, mountain, blue, trees, eyes, air, black, horse, rack (the scudding cloud-masses in the foreground that blot out the distant effects), and water. The first Latinical item is *vapor*, and not too decisive; but *citadel* accompanies *tower'd*, and *pendent* accompanies *rock; forked mountain* is not necessarily conscious of the Latinity of its second member, but presently there is *blue promontory*, clearly bi-lingual, and *promontory* (a fore-mountain) echoes *mountain*, and gives back to it its own Latinity: *black vesper's pageants* is a climactic compound ending Antony's first period. His second speech is a bi-lingual three-liner. Our interest is in *dislimns* followed by *indistinct* in the same line and even, though this looks unlikely, in the same sense. *Limn* is Latin-via-French, and *tinct* is Latin, both meaning draw or paint. The *dis-* of *dislimns* is privative; so is the *in-* of *indistinct* but not its *dis-*. (If it were, we should have in the word a double negative.) Here that prefix means "apart"; and the two words are fairly synonymous. Our attention focuses principally and longest on these two words in their curious and dangerous relation; and *indistinct* goes back and echoes *dislimns* just as *promontory* echoed *mountain*. The easy tone of the passage masks the achievement, the mastery, which is something of great intricacy.

Now a look at a very late passage of Shakespeare. It is from Prospero's speech when he is explaining to Miranda and Ferdinand the disappearance of the spirits in the midst of the mask which he has commanded; then moralizing the event for their instruction. If Prospero with his enchanter's wand in some sense represents Shakespeare with his dramatic imagination, the passage is Shakespeare's final utterance of his conviction of the general mortality, and his rueful sense

that, though life is handsome enough while we live it,
yet as its end draws near one sees that it never had a
solid substance.

> *Our revels now are ended. These our actors,*
> *As I foretold you, were all spirits, and*
> *Are melted into air, into thin air;*
> *And, like the baseless fabric of this vision,*
> *The cloud-capp'd towers, the gorgeous palaces,*
> *The solemn temples, the great globe itself,*
> *Yea, all which it inherit, shall dissolve,*
> *And, like this insubstantial pageant faded,*
> *Leave not a rack behind. We are such stuff*
> *As dreams are made on; and our little life*
> *Is rounded with a sleep.*

The vision disappeared, and so it will be with the
world itself, and ourselves. This is said with some
pretty doubling between the vernacular and the
Latinity; as if one had better deal with it now one way
and again the other way, that is, playfully, gracefully,
not too grimly and willfully. The two versions thoroughly interpenetrate each other, though the vernacular is the main one. The actors of the masque *are
melted into air*, which is a folkish disposition, and
there is a folkish addition in *into thin air*. Yet this same
masque is described below as a *vision* made of a *base-
less fabric*. The world with its objects and people will
dissolve (a variation on *melt*) like the *vision*, which
becomes an *insubstantial pageant* (whose *melted* appears now as *faded*). The contents of the world are
identified by four objects, of which the middle two
are *gorgeous palaces* and *solemn temples*, with *cloud-
capped towers* and *the great globe itself* on the two
sides; and the people are *all which it inherit*. The last
three lines, after the high-toned *insubstantial pageant*,
are in solid vernacular. Our substance is a *stuff* (the

equivalent of *fabric*), but the stuff of dreams; that is to say, our life is a dream, and the dream is set in the midst of the long sleep out of which it rises and into which it goes. Would we have this peculiar "view of life" elaborated? It is put better in the vernacular (for the most part) than it could have been put Latinically, or technically, because then the staple would be the philosophical language, and it might be expected to account for itself better. The dream-business uses two common poetic figures; thus, life is but a dream; and not only that, death is but a sleep; so that the dream-idea has a sleep-idea to depend on.

Since these words of Prospero are almost Shakespeare's last words to us, I will not stop without one more remark. Prospero has addressed them to Ferdinand and Miranda, who do not seem particularly appalled; their own dream is just coming to its head. When next we shall discover them, they will be playing at chess and love, and presently, when all the characters come in, Miranda will say:

> *O wonder!*
> *How many goodly creatures are there here!*
> *How beauteous mankind is! O brave new world,*
> *That has such people in it!*

To which Prospero will reply drily:

> *'Tis new to thee.*

Prospero will make his plans to go back with the company to Naples for the wedding, and then to retire to his Milan, where

> *Every third thought shall be my grave.*

His dream has at least had a good ending, and it is time for another dream. Would it not be gross of us to wish different theological views upon Prospero? Since these are in character, and dramatically adequate, we should do well to cultivate Keats's "negative capability," and let well enough alone.

One of the forms that negative capability might take with a poet would be this: to pass slyly back and forth between his two languages, if he is an English poet; as if he could not be expected to arrive at systematic theology with such a variable instrument.

EMPIRICS IN POLITICS [1]

Abook thirty political theorists figure in Mr. Kirk's big book. He picked them as the most distinguished examples of the conservative mind, and it was to be expected that they would be very unequal in the degrees of their distinction. Mr. Kirk himself is no common conservative, but a religious humanist, and it seems that he would like to recover to conservatism the whole body of doctrine as Burke delivered it to the moderns. Perhaps half of these figures are equipped almost as he would have them; the number is surprising. Practically all are British or American. For the fact must be as Mr. Kirk states it: among all the nations the English-speaking ones have conserved their polities the best, and it is their statesmen who should know how this is done. Exceptional in the series are only Tocqueville the Frenchman, who made himself conversant with both these polities, and was of a congenial temperament; and Spanish Santayana, who lived many years at Cambridge, Massachusetts, without coming any nearer to liking our heretical American mores. Mr. Kirk presents his figures by a good method, letting them speak for themselves in part, then resuming them and rounding them off; his own language may seem a little too resonant sometimes, but perhaps is not more so than that of the originals.

The difference between a total conservatism, like that of Burke and Kirk, and the campaigning conserv-atism that we are more familiar with, is that the one has a pragmatic doctrine and a theological doctrine,

[1] *The Conservative Mind. From Burke to Santayana.* By Russell Kirk. Regnery.

and the other has only a pragmatic doctrine. There should be a good deal of interest in Mr. Kirk's theologism and humanism, but the only practical attitude he expresses toward the Leviathan of modern business is a dull hatred. This is not statesmanlike, and in fact it is simply not possible as the attitude of a political party that means to take part in public affairs. There is no grappling, so far as he is concerned, with the economic responsibilities which a government has to undertake nowadays even if it is a conservative government. For instance, John Maynard Keynes figures in this book only as the name of a man who wrote *Two Memoirs* and said that the Benthamite calculus had been obstructive to the advancement of political theory. I can imagine many of Mr. Kirk's readers saying to themselves: Exactly; the conservatives have no taste for the modern economy, and the only role that is open to them is to let their enemies make the laws, and to hope that at some time they may take over the government themselves in order to administer them.

Burke lived before the age of mass production; he was an able economist, complimented by Adam Smith himself; but he could not know of either the difficulty or the necessity of securing by legislation a precisely adequate mass consumption, at whatever cost to conservative principles. We are familiar with the simple practical argument of Burke's on behalf of sticking to an existing order of society when its economy was simpler: it is an old order, which has come to represent the accrued wisdom of the ages, and so is necessarily superior to the opposed wisdom of our own single age; and it is the one among all possible orders under which its members may know by actual experience that they can support life and happiness. But it was a point of doctrine with Burke also to defend it theologically; as the order which came into being in the inscrutable and divinely ordained historic process, and must be so acknowledged by religious persons. Unfortunately, the conservatives do not always win their case against the innovators, and then the question rises of whether they have properly understood the divine laws of history. Indeed, since Burke, history would seem to have brought the conservatives to defeat in a long succession of engagements. They cannot but count these occasions as defeats, and setbacks for mankind; but on the other hand they usually accept the result. We may see in our country in this year of 1953 how conservatives when they return to power do not proceed heroically to undo the innovations of their enemies, as they may have threatened they would; but acquiesce in them, almost without a word of explanation, as if another chapter of history had been written irrevocably. The consequence is, to be sure, that history has been written, and the given chapter finished and laid by, since the conservatives are not going to challenge it. But a conservative historian cannot then treat of certain epochal events without some embarrassment. Suppose Mr. Kirk is dealing with the famous Reform Bills of 1832, 1867, and 1884, which extended the franchise and made the whole English people at least potentially the sovereign. His imagination cannot be restrained from playing on the issue as if it were still undecided, and he takes a sweet savor from the speeches and writings of his recalcitrant old Tories; but he recovers as a matter of course his sense of the Reform immediately afterward as an accomplished and sanctified historic event, which must be swallowed with whatever savor and without making too many faces. Reflecting upon the Reform of 1832, Mr. Kirk gives the theory of the conservative reconcilement with history, in language quite Burkean, yet touching all the same for its circumspectness:

Burke, and the better men among his disciples, knew that change in society is natural, inevitable, and beneficial; the statesman should not struggle vainly to dam the whole stream of alteration, because that would be opposing Providence; instead, his duty is to reconcile innovation and prescriptive truth, to lead the waters of novelty into the canals of custom. This accomplished, even though he may seem to himself to have failed, the conservative has executed his destined work in the great mysterious incorporation of the human race [which is Burke's own term for the concrete conservative state]; and if he has not preserved intact the old ways he loved, still he has moderated greatly the ugly aspect of new ways.

And when a party is prepared to accommodate itself to the stream of alteration even after resisting it, that would seem much to the public advantage. Evidently the badge which the conservative wears must have two faces. One is resistance to the new event; this is the fighting face, the one that ordinarily we choose to know him by. The other is acceptance after the event, permitting the expectation that when once the new ways are shaken down and become old ways they too will be loved. And that would argue a saving ultimate good sense. This party is of course not a revolutionary one; but we should see that it is not even, exactly, a counter-revolutionary one. It is—in the English-speaking countries—a civil party.

But still it looks like a mechanical service, or at least a rather menial one, if the party is to offer itself simply as a brake against alteration; it is hard to discover in that role enough of specific intelligence to qualify it as a religiosity of high grade. And when the alteration comes to pass nevertheless, is there a piety humanly capable of the enthusiastic reversal that is in order?

For example, is it pious of Mr. Kirk to testify that change is beneficial though its aspect is ugly? Perhaps he means that change as change is mere becoming, therefore hideous, but change accomplished passes into true being and is fit for the contemplation of the blessed. But I think not. And to what benefit does he refer? It would seem as if the conservatives had declined on principle, even after the event, to identify the precise benefit, which would be as if they were confessing an error in their precedent piety. Or is the divine process so inscrutable that the best of men cannot be sure of understanding it? In that case they might have presented their views with greater moderation. But there are naughty possibilities in Mr. Kirk's statement. He does not sufficiently deter godless men from the inference that Providence may have been compromising with evil, and using the decent conservatives as His agents in getting the best terms possible. On the whole, it would seem risky to invoke theological sanctions for one's politics; it is a game that two can play at; better still, it is a game that does not have to be played at all.

It may be that my representations do not do full justice to Mr. Kirk's argument (though I think they nearly do), but at any rate they have not considered the most interesting part of Burke's argument, which is something very special, or perhaps it is unique. Burke was a poor Irishman by birth, a citizen of one of the most wretched countries of the period; but he had no sooner got his schooling than he hurried off to be an Englishman, by adoption. He had exactly the perspective for appreciating the excellence of English institutions, and the fresh style of the new convert for defending them, amidst the rancor and strife of old-line politicians. The English state must have been superior then to anything on earth in its peculiar kind: it was old, and had grown consistently along its own lines, and in latter times so peacefully that even the Revolution of 1688 could be just barely regarded as an event without violence enough really to break the continuity. It was easy for the pious Burke to regard it with a religious passion. This nation was a "great mysterious incorporation of the human race" under God's hand. (It has not been easy for Americans to have such feelings about their own nation, whose constitution was so obviously a human artifact; though Mr. Kirk would have us attempt it in our degree.) The English nation in one way and another, whether quite independently of human contrivance or through the tender nurture of the wise rulers, had come down through the ages to what it was for Burke then; with its crown, church, aristocracy, property, and happy though unequal subjects. As for venerating it, that was quite according to another understanding, a broader one, which religious persons at that time were well acquainted with. Man does not know God immediately, and will understand His mind and plan only by studying the order of nature which He has instituted for man's instruction and happiness. (Many persons in the eighteenth century appear to have said that; it was a poet who said it most handsomely, under the eighteenth-century title of "An Essay on Man.") But one of the institutions in the universal order, perhaps even the most notable one, was that natural and orderly institution, the English state. Its rate of alteration had been so slow! A little alteration at a time, so that it had never broken the pattern; that was hardly the history of a human production. And the statesman had only to preserve the constitution of this state as he had received it. By no means was he to reason freshly about it; he had his own natural and proper prejudice, a far better guide, to go by. It was the reasoning of the *philosophes* in England's neighbor state which produced the horrors of the French Revolution. The impact of that upon Burke was almost excessive at sixty years of age. He reacted with a grand rage, and wrote the incomparable *Reflections*, a book which is required reading for students of politics, and which most of us know anyhow as the place where the conception of the English state is aired with wonderful spirit, and documented prodigiously.

Burke trusted his own experience of the English state, which was in plain view and entirely accessible. His is an empirical faith, the religious counterpart of falling in love with what is nearest to you and most domesticated yet most wonderful. We are moved to ask about Burke's relation to John Locke, the father of English philosophical empiricism. It is held by political theorists that he owed a great deal to Locke; and for example, the idea of the social contract, which may be only tacit and virtual, or may be written, but in which at any rate the rulers undertake to protect the interest of the ruled, and the ruled undertake to obey their rulers. But Burke departed from Locke in maintaining that, at least in the politics of this ancient and happy England, it was better to consult prejudice than reason. Locke believed in knowing the natural order, and adapting to it in general, but also in reasoning from it boldly if one knows how. The productive arts and sciences, for instance, are empirical because, characteristically, they reason from artificial dispositions of nature, or contrived experiments; but they come back if not to original nature then to re-formed nature, which is supposed to be even better. It is unfortunate that the Greek root from which a whole family of terms is taken means, indifferently, either experience or experiment. So there are two faces to empiricism. One is the process of fresh experiment, atomizing nature and re-combining it; the other is the appeal to the routine of ordinary experience because there is already a fixation upon some familiar object so good that it must never be let go. Burke in his politics came under the second. In a "Letter to a Member of the National Assembly" he has a fantastic image of the French leaders being advised to keep their Revolution going even after there have been some bad disappointments:

> But the *charlatan* tells them that what is passed cannot be helped;—they have taken the draught, and they must wait its operation with patience;— that the first effects indeed are unpleasant, but that the very sickness is a proof that the dose is of no sluggish operation;—that sickness is inevitable in all constitutional revolutions;—that the prescriber is not an empiric who proceeds by vulgar experience, but one who grounds his practice on the sure rules of art, which cannot possibly fail.

The charlatan here is an experimental empiric, but Burke accepts for himself the scornful designation of "an empiric who proceeds by vulgar experience." He meant to be just that. Burke in politics goes by the large commonplaces of experience.

So, Mr. Kirk's book teaches, do many other conservative statesmen. And if the statesman's experience is with an ancient polity which God Himself has ordained, there is a fair presumption that he is an English statesman. We seem to have here a special historic conformation of Mr. Kirk's title-subject, the conservative mind. Once I had my chance to make this observation at first hand. The Oxford college which accepted me as a Rhodes Scholar undergraduate just before the first World War was one that liked to take its Americans from the Southern states, on the supposition that they were the more "English." And before long I was glad to accept an invitation to join the most conservative of those college clubs which were given to debating the questions of the day after the fashion of a Parliament. But I came to have a function in the debates which I had not counted on. The questions proposed were often such that only one side was fit for a decent conservative to support, and the Honorable Secretary would have trouble finding a spokesman for the bad or liberal side. Now an American was scarcely expected to be solemnly committed in his views by hereditary convictions. Soon I was doing much more than my share of the debating, and always on the losing side, which was only in part because I was not equal to the passion or the style of the young statesmen. I can recall almost verbatim the following passage in one debate.

> *Mover of the Question:*—I may as well say, Sir, that I am a Tory, and I take that to mean that I am dedicated with all my being to the defense first of my Sovereign, and then of my Church.
> *Interruption from the Floor:*—Shame, Sir! Do you not think a Tory is obligated to defend the Empire?
> *Mover:*—I accept the gentleman's rebuke and thank him for reminding me. I am dedicated to the defense, thirdly, of the Empire.

I felt that this was the conservative mind in its flower. But it brought me a sudden great relief to reflect that I was not dedicated to any such defenses, but was free, and in the nature of the case was excused. I had not been born to it, and could not possibly repair the omission.

We must be tempted to find this same conservative quality (empiric in the second or vulgar sense) in the English feeling for many other of the inherited patterns of English life besides politics; for the English manners, cookery, houses, landscaping, sports, fashions, clubs; where we may say at least that there is a prejudice in favor of old ways in preference to reasoned and strange ways; even though the sentiment may not be of a dignity to acquire a felt religious sanction. (The difference sometimes looks very slight.) And how English! the foreigner has sometimes said; often, How charming! when the faith was surely founded; or, for that matter, when it was founded sufficiently, and professed spontaneously and without guile. That the English life has been happily conducted on this basis may be attributed, if one is not too strict to make compliments, to a special grace vouchsafed to this people by Providence; it may be said that the English are a highly favored people, and have taken good care to deserve it.

Very well. But one cannot quite think that this temper prevails in England now. For various reasons; but surely one reason is both cogent and of great honor: because it has proved too hard to maintain a lyrical and empirical eighteenth-century euphoria against a certain importunate modern ghost. I mean the guilt-feeling, or harsh Categorical Imperative, or voice of God itself, or whatever you may call the impalpable thing, which compels the nations to make their peace with their constitutions as best they can and repair the bleak situations and minds of their un-propertied citizens. Has there been since early Christianity a moral impulse so unqualified and unequivocal? It has a way of penetrating all the systems of politics, and where it is not accommodated (as it appears to be "by Providence" in the English-speaking countries) it shatters them.

Burke's total conservatism is scarcely recoverable now. There is nothing climactic in Mr. Kirk's concluding chapter, "The Recrudescence of Conservatism," but only a confusion of ringing ambitious passages. He is still saying Burke, but actually he wants the conservatives to appropriate the very reforms against which they have fought and advance them under the party colors. The idea is startling at first. But we ought to say gladly: Let them do it. It must often have happened that conservatives, whose acceptance comes after the event, have confiscated their enemies' political estate and administered it very well. And this brings me back to the point where I started. The conservative mind is not unable, as has been charged, to learn any lesson from the changes of history. It is only unable to recite the lesson faithfully.

WHY CRITICS DON'T GO MAD

It gives me a mild astonishment when I discover that critics of poetry do not really go mad. That seems to be the honorable prerogative of the poets, in whose train the critics follow, though not so far as that. But the critics have a great and public stake in poetry, and in the fate of those fluent existences, epiphanies, and "levels of meaning" which poets call into being. Especially the modern critic; who thinks he must know the ultimate reality of the poetic visions, and who may say if he likes that his precursor, the ur-modern, was Coleridge, whose inquiries into the nature of poetry were frankly metaphysical, or religious. So our gifted critic will get himself quickly into the intangibles of the subject, and thence into metaphysics, that universe which it is very hard to traverse, where the treacherous skies seem always about to thin out and clear, and the jostling elements seem about to precipitate their solid substances and assume fixed places. But these are events which do not readily occur, at least without the benefit of dogma which makes them occur. To the modern critic (who is perhaps among the most presentable instances of modern man) the ancient religious establishments may seem to have thought they found their solid ground too easily; it is as if religion took it for granted that it had achieved its form and station once and forever, yet still there had to come a "modern" time when everything was called into question and religion had to start all over again at the speculative level; and the second speculation is bound to be more hazardous than the first. But at any rate the critic in his own speculations is going to have many a moment asking himself if he sees what he thinks he sees, and means what he says he means, and if this is really the life for him. There is a bad sense of lostness, made the worse because he cannot take his trusting readers into his confidence. And now comes the period when he awakens in the night and tosses on his bed. It is when I think of his pains at this stage that I wonder why madness does not come to his aid. Heaven does not appear to accord so blank and absolute a relief to the critic, but only one that is humane and probationary. What happens is very sudden: an explosion of laughter, as the honest critic confesses that he cannot support his great ambitions, let other critics support theirs or not as may be; after which he will turn over and sleep like a babe, to awaken to bird-calls by daylight like a man restored, for the time being. The critic's happiness is not even contaminated by any need to make a public confession. But his next ensuing essays almost make up by the modesty of their range what they lack, to the surprise of his regular readers, in the old daring and subtlety.

It will be apparent that I think of the critic very certainly as a good man; a man of integrity pursuing an uncertain career. He will not go mad. And parents may be advised, if they ask advice, that they need not fear to entrust the good young men their sons to him at the university, if they can qualify for the courses. They will be made acquainted among other things with the soul of man, and even the soul of modern man, and that is something which is in store for them anyhow, one time or another.

Mr. Cleanth Brooks has for some years, I think, been teaching Milton to a *corps d'élite* of pupils, and now he and Mr. Hardy have collaborated in getting out a new book in exegesis of the Minor Poems.[1] I shall be

[1] *Poems of Mr. John Milton.* The 1645 Edition, with Essays and Analysis by Cleanth Brooks and John Edward Hardy, 1952.

referring entirely, as I believe, to Mr. Brooks's part of this book. This is the early Milton, but already he is a serious poet; I think we may as well say he is a religious poet. And Brooks has advanced steadily in seriousness, and here will be thought of partly as a religious critic.

It seems to me that Brooks just now is probably the most forceful and influential critic of poetry that we have. But this does not imply that his authority is universally accepted, for it has turned out even better than that. Where he does not gain assent, he arouses protest and countercriticism. His tone toward other critics is that of an independent, and his tone toward scholars who are occasional critics is cool. This is why a new book by Brooks is a public service. The book on Milton will stir up some waters that may have grown brackish. There are likely to be requitals made upon Brooks by the rival critics and the scholars, but after that there will be soul-searching, and I shall not be surprised if it proves finally that Brooks will have touched off a Milton revival and caused our human and poetic understanding of this poet to reach a new level of intelligence.

And of course there will be readers who will go all the way with Brooks as if under a spell. I believe the peculiar fascination of his view of poetry is due to its being a kind of modern version of the ancient doctrine of divine inspiration or frenzy. For Brooks the poem exists in its metaphors. The rest of it he does not particularly remark. He goes straight to the metaphors, thinking it is they which work the miracle that is poetry; and naturally he elects for special notice the most unlikely ones. Hence paradox and irony, of which he is so fond. Now if you count little ones with big ones the two figures must be about as ubiquitous as any we have; they are easy to find once you are searching for them. It is paradox when you find something which in its bearing looks both ways, pro and con, good and bad; irony when you have something you thought was firmly established . in the favorable sense, as good, and pro, but discover presently that it has gone bad for you, and is contra; the one is a pregnant ambiguity, the other is a radical yet slightly humorous sense of disappointment where you had least reason to expect it. The instances may be petty, and indeed the paradoxes may be only the accidents of words. But now and then there will be a paradox or an irony which is vivid, and crucial too, for great issues turn on it. So, and rightly, Brooks pounces. Then he proceeds to wrestle as much of the poem as possible under it as the "dominating" figure; it is likely to have philosophical or religious implications; and there is his sense of the poem. I do not seem able to describe the procedure without making it seem capricious. Brooks's method, however, is a homiletic one if I am not mistaken. In my boyhood I heard many a sermon preached where the preacher unpacked the whole burden of his theology from a single figurative phrase of Scripture taken out of context. Brooks heard them too. The fact is that Brooks and I were about as like as two peas from the same pod in respect to our native region, our stock (we were sons of ministers of the same faith, and equally had theology in our blood), the kind of homes we lived in, the kind of small towns; and perhaps we were most like in the unusual parallel of our formal educations. So we have more in common than we can have acquired separately. If we have diverged a little for the moment, perhaps it is only because now our habitations are far apart.

Brooks's particular theologism resembles that of Scotus, who preached as all critics know the individuality or *haecceitas* of the well-regarded object. He does not want the poem to have a formal shape, but simply

to unfold its own metaphorical energy; at least this
is the impression we will take from his theoretical discussions and many of his applied criticisms. And it
will follow that you, the reader, must not recite in
your own prose the action that takes place in entirely
different terms in the poem. (The *quidditas* is not the
haecceitas, the "paraphrase" is not the poem.) If you
do you may be swept away into the ultimate depravity
where all the readers have only a "scientific" intelligence. But what have we here? I believe that here is
precisely where the modern criticism came in: in the
new (or rediscovered) sense that the poetic object
must be defended in its full and private being. A
reasonable dictum might be that the modern criticism
came in with Croce. Did not his American disciple
Spingarn present him in this country in 1911 with a
book entitled *The New Criticism?* But many critics
now thought they could assimilate this revelation and
go on. If the poem has to be defended in the wholeness
of its being, what of that character in the poem
which makes it discourse? In whatever terms, the
poem has generality and definition, if anybody wants
them; it remains, if the grammarian looks at it, a species
of Aristotelian discourse. Thus it has a beginning,
middle, and end, if the argument is sizeable enough to
bother about such things; and otherwise there is the
"point" of the poem, the act of predication, or the
sheer core-object, with such qualifications as may
appear; and everywhere that minute kind of order
which we call syntax, not fatally overlaid or con-
cealed. To so much logical formalism the metaphors
and brilliances have to adapt, and surely it is very
advantageous for them. They have two natures in one,
and Brooks should be delighted by that paradox. A
poem in itself is one of the most various objects in the
world; and this is besides the limitless variety between
one poem and another. Twenty critics will enter the

same poem and come out with twenty different reports; yet every one may be right, even the one who has found only a "moral," or a doctrine of faith. Are we going to defend this poem by locking it up against people who want their vital but vulgar "uses" of it? And should we do something about locking up nature likewise? Nor is the poem destroyed by use any more than nature is. I catch myself saying this over and over, and conclude that I have a bump of discretion bigger than Brooks has, and really an ignominious deformity.

As for the learned scholars, they have their own proprietary interest in the poem. I am worried lest the critic may not receive the whole benefit of them, or at any rate the benefit of the rare and elect spirits among them. Now criticism is literary judgment; and learning, though it is nonpareil in respect of possessing its "facts," may have very little of that character. Yet there is a possibility. Brooks will take his critical method and put it to work with a fury and a spate of words; I in my degree have been ready with a gabble of my own. But at my shoulder I have sometimes seemed to sense a strong silent presence attending and watching me. It is not Virgil, for he attends the poets; this Guide for the critics, as I sense his presence, is the Great Scholar, so modest that he is anonymous, and in my vision I have never been able to identify him; but perfect in his attainments; possessing the sense of the art as wholly as he possesses the text, in beautiful proportion and justice, yet intuitively, without an effort; it is precisely because he has been a faithful scholar that this grace has been added unto him. He causes me to be apprehensive that my kind of criticism may be so partial as to belittle the poem, for he will know it at once, and it will be painful to see him register his embarrassment. Is he the figment of a bad conscience? I do not know if he exists in our time. But he ought to. And then comes a consideration which is a deplorable anticlimax: I wish he might have also, nowadays, a little of our gift of gab, Brooks's and mine; the better to make his admonishing presence felt to the young men rushing into criticism.

One of the items of the 1645 Edition is, of course, that popular pair, *L'Allegro* and *Il Penseroso;* and here Brooks's analysis is a hold-over from the book of five years ago, *The Well Wrought Urn.* For once, Brooks runs pretty well through the lengthy argument of the pieces. It is not according to his rule, before the present book at least, but he can do it under color of giving the views of the other critics. His dialectic as he goes along has a great deal of animation; and I will not forget to say that this essay is the best writing I have seen on the paired poems. But at last Brooks elects the decisive figure which he thinks will hold everything together. It is the figure of light-vs.-shadow, with the shadow which pervades *Il Penseroso* really brighter than the light of *L'Allegro;* and Brooks has made a strong bid. The text which supports the paradox is a passage near the beginning of *Il Penseroso* describing the goddess Melancholy:

> *Whose Saintly visage is too bright*
> *To hit the Sense of human sight;*
> *And therfore to our weaker view,*
> *Ore laid with black staid Wisdom's hue.*

Brooks explains that "the black of night, 'staid Wisdom's hue,' is merely a necessary veil to conceal a brightness in reality too intense for human sight." Then he boldly connects this passage with the passage near the very end, where the pleasures of the melancholy man grow decidedly religious, and turn on his seeing the "dimm religious light" of the church windows. The dimness of the religious light is an anti-Platonic image which seems to me entirely Miltonic.

And it is much to my own taste. (I am hurt by the glare to which Plato's philosophers coming out of the human cave are subjected; or for that matter Dante's Pilgrim coming perilously close to his Heavenly Vision; even in imagination my eyes cannot take it.)

Brooks's essay is so good, and his election of the one big metaphor so striking, that I do not mean to enter any more of my pedantic objections, but only to ask for something more from him. After all, the essay which suited its original purpose has been transferred to a book having to present things which would spoil a formal essay, even more an informal one. One of the favorite theses of the book is the contention that Milton is not so close to the Spenserian school stylistically as he has generally been put, and closer to the so-called "metaphysical"; which he argues at a number of places by showing that beneath the "marmoreal surface" of Milton's verse there is an energy of language which is not Spenserian at all, but more like metaphysical. Now it has been said that Brooks's criticism provokes Brooks's critics to criticism; very well. The jog-trot of the two poems here, putting the Jolly Man and the Pensive Man through their paces, is very informal indeed, and we would say that it is relaxed, if we did not have something that only a meticulous labor could have achieved: the close methodical cross-references continually from one poem to the other. The tetrameter lines do not have the logical tightness of metaphysical poetry, the couplets scarcely have the logical definition of couplets, and the composition in its parts and as a whole is not metaphysical. It jingles. The earlier poem on the Marchioness of Winchester seems at least to have been conceived metaphysically. It begins,

> *This rich Marble doth enterr*
> *The honour'd Wife of Winchester,*
> *A Viscount's daughter, an Earls heir,*

but it quickly loses its metaphysical headway, and Brooks observes acutely that Milton's failure with this and a few other poems may have helped "to estrange him from the explicitly 'conceited' and witty poetry of Donne." I am suggesting that there might be a comparison between Milton's tetrameter couplets and those of a metaphysical poet, without reference to the witty conceits. And suppose we glance at the "Horatian Ode" of Milton's friend Marvell, though that came twenty years or so later. Marvell scores a great success with his meters there, and doubles his triumph by composing his stanza out of a pair of tetrameters followed by a pair of trimeters! A *tour de force* in the short style. I quote several stanzas, which of course are not to be taken as consecutive:

> *So restless Cromwell could not cease*
> *In the inglorious arts of peace,*
> > *But through adventurous war*
> > *Urged his active star. . . .*

> *Could by industrious valor climb*
> *To ruin the great work of time,*
> > *And cast the kingdom old*
> > *Into another mould. . . .*

> *That thence the royal actor borne*
> *The tragic scaffold might adorn;*
> > *While round the armed bands*
> > *Did clap their bloody hands.*

> *He nothing common did or mean*
> *Upon that memorable scene,*
> > *But with his keener eye*
> > *The axe's edge did try.*

In these stanzas the metaphysical effect does not depend particularly upon wit, nor yet upon the well-known extended conceit employed by the school. It is an effect possible to poets who are weighty yet idiomatic; polite conversationalists, perhaps, who do not have to make speeches in order to offer important observations. This style we should have to describe as a "grave" or "pithy" style, as distinguished from the "full" or "periodic" or Spenserian style. Marvell was strong yet supple to the point that he could turn on a sixpence; or at any rate a florin. Milton did not like to have his movement cramped. He liked his swelling periods, which at the same time are going to be more compacted than Spenser's. His most idiomatic style is probably to be found in the occasional secular sonnets, some of which have no equals in our language.

Milton did not manage his tetrameters with metaphysical skill. But in the very first of his important poems he had a fling at the couplet of trimeters, and it is most engaging. Perhaps the trimeters compelled him to break the long pentameter stride to which he was already becoming habituated, as the tetrameters did not quite because they were so near to pentameters. I quote from the "Hymn," composed at the age of twenty-one:

> *And sullen* Moloch *fled,*
> *Hath left in shadows dred,*
> *His burning Idol all of blackest hue,*
> *In vain with Cymbals ring,*
> *They call the grisly king,*
> *In dismal dance about the furnace blue,*
> *The brutish gods of* Nile *as fast,*
> Isis *and* Orus, *and the Dog* Anubis *hast.*

But Milton here is not risking all on the trimeter couplets. They take the stage jauntily, and speak up clearly, but the scene has not really been turned over to them. The long lines are always waiting to step forward and complete what they have started. It is needless to say that it is all very beautiful, and one could hardly have predicted at this moment what the new poet was going to do.

It is my impression that the metaphysical poets have a sharper metrical sense, and can do more work with it, than most other poets of English; and that the reader to whom they do not communicate this sense is missing badly. I have intimated that they do not jingle. But often they will jangle; and by premeditation, for that is one way of advertising the metrical form of the compostition. Thus,

All whom the flood did, and fire shall, o'erthrow,

which comes from the poet who cheerfully submitted to the critical opinion that he "deserved hanging for not keeping of accents." There are even more startling instances, but I choose this because it is the line of an obvious sonnet and therefore as everybody knows must rate as an iambic pentameter. The good reader of poetry does not live who can come to this line for the first time and not re-read it, once or three times, before he has got the music and can pass on. It is one of the special incidents of the grave style. It has the musical quality of counterpoint; there is conflict between the powerful though irregular rhythms of the phrases and the metronome beat of the meter; it proves to be of advantage to both sides, for the phrase-rhythms refused to be muffled, yet the meter goes marching on.

In the Marvell stanzas which I have quoted above there is neither jingle nor jangle, but there is a tightness; and what there must not be is any sense on our part of what has been prettily called a "felicity" of diction; not if the term would indicate our feeling that the meters were not very hard taskmasters anyhow, and the phrases had managed to fit in without the slightest trouble. It is depressing when a reader tells us how very "natural" the meters seem. For it would then be as if the meters, or the poetic understanding which thought it was respecting the meters, were ceasing to function, and the meters did not know their own importance. Meters activated, as they are when the metaphysicals use them, seem at first to be restrictive, and obstructive, upon the flow of the language, but actually they are what makes the phrases shine. The Marvell lines individually, if we could now isolate them in imagination, *i.e.*, as independent bits of language on their own, too short to be identified as anything but prose, may well have very little distinction; those of the second quoted stanza are in a rhetorical commonplace. But that is not our sense of them as they stand.

At this point I would propose a certain wide and over-all conception of the poem. A little while ago I was urging Brooks to acknowledge the logical form of the poem as something fixed and—for the hard-headed English-speaking public—invincible; which the showy metaphors, episodic or "dominant" as they might be, had better make their peace with, especially since it would do them no harm; and I had the idea of a poem as a great "paradox," a construct looking two ways, with logic trying to dominate the metaphors, and metaphors trying to dominate the logic, and neither, or both (as we have it in paradoxes), succeeding. But now I suggest that we must reckon with the meters too, and the poem assumes the form of a trinitarian existence. For the meters in turn enforce themselves against the logic and the metaphors, but against resistance. Since Brooks likes such terms as "equilibrium" and "organic structure," I am proposing still handsomer effects, in that family of effects, than even he has allowed for.

But by this reckoning the stock of the metaphysicals would go pretty high, and might that not be a danger to the position of Shakespeare, or the position of Milton? I believe not. If Brooks and I were being landed on the desert island, I have no doubt that the books we would severally take along would be the same books, and chosen in the same order, and we would read them in unison. The metaphysicals achieved a high lyric perfection; such a rounded and many-way perfection, I imagine, as a Dante essayist might attribute to Dante if Dante had been their compatriot and had lived in the early seventeenth century—though I do not know anything about Dante's counterpointing. But the metaphysicals could not write epics, nor plays. And here again we have a great and proper equilibrium, such as a humanist must like very much. Every poet finds his place in the company of poets, and there is no necessity for killing one poet to make room for another.

THE CONCRETE UNIVERSAL: OBSERVATIONS ON THE UNDERSTANDING OF POETRY

M Y TITLE employs a famous working-phrase of Hegel's, and already I have made some lay observations about that philosopher's understanding of poetry.[1] But Hegel's thought is a special development of Kant's, and the fact is that I am obliged to think of Kant as my own mentor. Kant is closer to our critical feeling than Hegel is! So I shall talk of Kant's understanding of poetry, and at even greater length. But perhaps a small apologia is in order, perhaps it is already overdue,—for bringing philosophy into the literary discussion.

I don't know how it is possible to deny to the literary critic the advantages of philosophy; I suppose we have fears that he, or his audience, will be unequal to them. But does he not try for a radical and decisive understanding of poetry? I could believe that he should be denied if I thought it must follow that, having once got into philosophy, he would never get out again. This would mean that resiliency had gone for some reason from his working consciousness, that the fateful time had come when the usual succession of its moods and interests must break down; which would be distressing if it did not seem arbitrary.

Probably the critic's ordinary job is to interpret the poem in common language that is not philosophical, and does not stray far from the literary text. We think of him as trying to induce the right public reception of the poem when he has come straight from his own

[1] The present paper was published in the *Kenyon Review* as the second of a series of papers under one title.

experience of it. And we think his performance will be a little barbarous if some of the warmth of the object does not carry over into his presentation, and even some of the graces of its language.

The reading of technical philosophy is the critic's home work. It should be fruitful of radical and decisive ideas—if his mind is strong enough to take them. But can he afford to immerse his mind in the stiff and graceless language? He will be safe if his passion for his art is incorruptible. Indeed, the whole intention is to save him from unconscious errors, like some cheapening of the poem's effect, or some wretched exclusions that he might feel inclined to make within its meaning,—which would be like having the lie within his soul, more killing than jargon, if we must compare one evil with another. The philosophical understanding of poetry as we have it now is almost entirely a thing that has been achieved by the moderns; Concrete Universal is one of its key phrases. But even here the philosophers do not speak with one voice; as doubtless they never will. It is the critic's privilege to have a mind of his own when caught in the disagreements among the doctors. And he has at least one enormous advantage over the philosophers: he is intimate, and it must be very rare if they are intimate, with the immediate pulsing fact which is his poem. He scarcely needs to accept a philosophical disposition of his poem which seems not to have very much to do with the felt reality of the thing. Must he then assume the burden of being a critic of philosophy as well as literature? But the added labor does not mean the doubling of his burden. His single role is still the understanding of poetry, and while this is made surer and firmer it is really being made easier.

I suppose we can scarcely say that philosophy as a part of the critical discipline is according to Arnold, or even according to Eliot. It is according to Richards, and it is according to Coleridge. I find it pleasant to believe that the special revival of Coleridge in our time, in our language, signifies that critics direct their thought again to the heroic time when Augustan poetry, with its intricate surfaces and its abhorrence of passion, had played itself out finally, and was being succeeded by the fresh concert of the Romantics; when the poets themselves were amateurs of philosophy, and aware of the late or even the living philosophers of their art. The new philosophy was German. Schiller was its best spokesman in Germany among the poets and critics, and Coleridge, though scarcely Schiller's equal in speculative force, was his counterpart in English. The great philosophical name, of course, was that of Kant. We are still under the domination of an aesthetic humanism which we must call either Kantian or Post-Kantian. And when we plunge into the first-rate sequence of poets which includes Wordsworth, Coleridge, Byron, Shelley, Keats, we at once gather the impression that they are purposeful, dedicated, even programmatic, to a degree hardly equaled by another set of individual poets living in a single age. They had a common preoccupation with a certain understanding of poetry, and they had got it partly from the literary critics, but more and more it tended to go back to Kant, or to those critics who had assimilated their own views to Kant's. Now it will be said that they had also a preoccupation with political freedom, and the politics of revolution. But this one was not so leading. Perhaps it is more intense than the other preoccupation in Byron, but the case is just reversed in Keats; and both preoccupations are strong in Shelley. At any rate, as we proceed we come much too soon, for our mood, to Tennyson, and feel a cooling-off of our spirits; the epoch must have gone already, for here the succession passes once more to the nondescript, the poet who has received many gifts from the Muses but must take a long time deciding what had best be done with them, —and there will not be anything particularly philosophical in his decision when he makes it.

A little later we come to Browning, and Browning has a great deal of the Romantic philosophy in his equipment. Whether he borrows or originates it I do not know, though the former seems the more likely; but at any rate there has been the break already, and we do not associate him with the movement.

Then there is the third Victorian poet, a Matthew Arnold, about whom we shall always have very mixed feelings. His beginnings may inspire us to fancy that Keats has come to life again. But there is quickly a breakdown, the Keatsian strain is stifled, as Arnold proceeds to argue himself out of the Romantic movement. The effect is to convert the author of "The Strayed Reveller," and of the Callicles part of "Empedocles," into an intellectual poet, or an academic poet; though he may still indulge himself occasionally in some nostalgic echo of his early self. Arnold criticized the Romantics because they "did not know enough"; in England they had then no proper "current of ideas" to nourish them. Let us say simply, Nobody knows enough; or hardly anybody. Let that be the ample blanket which will cover the Romantics; but it must cover Arnold too; he did not fail to acquaint himself with the German literary critics, but he did not take them in their Kantian phase. When he talks about poetry we know that Kant's firm understanding of it has never reached him, or at least that it has never touched him. The physical death of Keats at an early age is painful to us, but worse, perhaps, is the death of the poet in the living Arnold, and I for one, on the present occasion, will not be consoled by thinking of the value of the public man who emerged from the ruin. It is easy to agree that Arnold was the happiest of all the rhetoricians in our language who have dedicated themselves to the public cause; that is to say, the most engaging schoolmaster who ever teased and scolded his bad pupils into bothering about "the best that has been thought and uttered in the world." But Arnold was not congenitally interested in the radical and decisive thought (and utterance) of the philosophers.

Concrete Universal is a useful term for systematic philosophy. Hegel hit upon it, but Kant might easily have used it, and I think he would have explained scrupulously the difference if he should have used it for two different kinds of occasion. Let us return to the vernacular to clear up this term, if we think that the critic may feel a little bewildered by the technicality, but that it allows of being translated into something more commonplace with which he is bound to be familiar. A Universal in Hegel's favorite sense is any idea in the mind which proposes a little universe, or organized working combination of parts, where there is a whole and single effect to be produced, and the heterogeneous parts must perform their several duties faithfully in order to bring it about. Thus the formula of a chemical reaction; the recipe for a dish; the blueprint of a machine; or even, to the extent in which it is practicable, Newman's "idea of a university." It becomes a Concrete Universal when it has been materialized and is actually working. The Universal by itself is the design as it exists in the understanding, and if we ask what is the Concrete by itself we must say, I imagine, that it is the objective element in which the Universal in all its parts is to be materialized.

Nevertheless, when we read Kant and Hegel, it must occur to us that there appear to be two kinds of Concrete Universal which are radically distinct. First, as the easier one by far for us to follow, there is the

Concrete Universal as we find it exemplified a thousand times in the operations of applied science. We do not there raise a question which has agitated many recent literary critics when they think of a poem as a Concrete Universal: whether the Concrete or working Universal realizes in precise measure the blue-print, the Universal in the mind, or whether there is an unused remainder of the Concreteness. Science means to have its Concrete Universal just right, and has it so; and the crucial factor in getting it right would perhaps be the determination of the scientist, if he does not find the right parts already existing in the state of nature, to alter the materials he does find, till they become right; to compound them or purify them, grow them or manufacture them, fit them to size and shape, and so on; in the Universal as designed there are specifications which they must meet. So the parts of the finished Concrete Universal do have their logical blue-print perfection, as follows: Not one necessary part missing; nor one unnecessary part showing; nor a part showing which is either excessive or deficient in its action even though some one might be (by the carelessness of the designer, or the stubbornness of the material), and still not fail to do its work after a fashion.

If we insist that engines and scientific processes are never perfect, and as a matter of fact are continually being improved upon, the answer is that at any rate they are perfectible; and in particular that the scientists are free to make any possible use of nature to obtain the specified parts, and are not to be deterred by any sentimental regard for nature.

But it is odd that literary critics should claim, so many of them (they would be banking heavily on Aristotle the ancient critic), that this same rigorous organization obtains within a poem; that the Universal or logical plan of the poem is borne out perfectly in the sensuous detail which puts it into action; and that this Concrete is used up so completely in the service of the Universal that there is no remainder. I believe this notion could not have occurred to either Kant or Hegel, because of one radical consideration which must have seemed to them too obvious to dwell upon.

It has to do with the peculiar purpose of a poem, as compared with a scientific or practical operation. Kant offered a new version of the essential human history behind a poem, and Hegel accepted it without any particular question. Speaking broadly, we are given to saying that applied science attends busily to our explicit appetitive or organic needs, and a scientific Universal is a workable concept seen in that perspective. Now the Universal of the poem is a moral Universal. There is difficulty enough, as we are well aware, when we try to locate the common moral impulse in the animal perspective of human nature, and many humanists follow Kant in saying that it is a "higher" impulse and requires us ultimately to posit a Supreme Being and an eternal Moral Order, if we mean to find a steady perspective in which to regard it objectively. That is, the understanding of common morality takes some metaphysical speculation to accomplish; and at the least it requires of any understanding a far more radical and imaginative psychology and anthropology than existed in Kant's time. All the same, the moral Universal often enough is perfectly explicit; that is, when we are in a situation where we see our duty clearly, and do it without question. That is morality in action, and Kant has treated it firmly in his *Critique of Practical Reason*, second of the big books in his trilogy. In a moral action we treat other persons as ends, not means; and if we propose to confer material benefits upon them we shall have to treat nature as a means and not an end, precisely as the scientists or other practical people do in working their Universals.

And there might conceivably be a poetry aiming

simply at our moral improvement, representing the most exemplary behaviors in order to move us to like behaviors. Doubtless there actually is such a poetry; but Kant despises it if he notices it, and Hegel after him. A little less disreputable (less absurdly simple) would be a kind of poetry given to representing moral situations where it is difficult not so much to do one's duty, but to know just which among the several possibilities is the duty one must do; exemplary in its practical judgments, in the nicety of its distinction among the moral ideas. Here we come close to Hegel's weakness and, by the same token, to Hegel's strength. But still this is not poetry as Kant conceives it consistently, or as Hegel conceives it ideally.

The moral Universal whose Concrete embodiment is a poem is different in its technique from that moral Universal, or from any other practicable Universal, which exacts from nature its prescribed parts and goes to work with them. Its object in a poem is surely "reflective," but since that is a weak word let us say it is metaphysical, as we must construe it; it is of an elemental importance which we feel profoundly even if we do not easily identify it. But we may start with the technical distinction, which is this: the moral Universal of the poem does not use nature as a means but as an end; it goes out into nature not as a predatory conqueror and despoiler but as an inquirer, to look at nature as nature naturally is, and see what its own reception there may be. The moral Universal takes a journey into nature, so to speak, and the Concrete element is an area of nature existing in its natural conformations as these are given, and discovered, not a Concrete element which it means to ransack for materials which have already been prescribed. It is for this reason that it seems idle for literary critics to raise the question whether, within the traversed region of nature, the unpredictable and highly particular detail of the local "manifold of sense" is going to enter precisely and without remainder into the formal Universal. That is too much to expect. We shall be glad to settle for much less than that. The sort of hospitality offered to our moral Universal by the Concrete of the natural world will need to be convincing, if it is to do us any good, but on the other hand the Universal is a mannerly and modest sort of tourist. I shall have to go into that topic by stages; it is not an easy topic; it is Kant's topic, and he makes it very clear in principle, but does not offer many case-histories for the benefit of the weak laity's understanding of poetry.

Let me clear up my feeling with regard to Hegel, in order to continue the better with Kant. There is a temperamental difference between Kant and Hegel. I think of Hegel as a benign yet extremely aggressive spirit to whom we have to attribute at last an intention as ambitious and simple as the following: to push the moral Universal like any other common Universal out into the objective world, where it is to enforce its presence, and in doing so to make that world over, even if only a little at a time; it will amount finally to a reformation of nature, as when it takes the form of substituting modern urban life for the old agrarian life. Up to a certain point the new world will be the natural one, so long as its forms may seem suited to our primitive moral feeling. And poetry will record its happiest moments. But under the speed-up of the Universals, the moral pressure grows so brisk and demanding that the natural world simply becomes mechanized, or adapted, and made over, a pure convenience which in its own right is quite disregarded. There will be an endless evolution in the complexity of human society, in its manners and ideals, its institutions and states, and this is one way to make the best of our curious existence; it is a very muscular way. There will be no poetry at this stage, because no honor can be wasted on nature. Poetry has already had its day, says Hegel. He speaks with a proud candor of the beauty which vanished with the classical arts (when even deities were anthropomorphic and could be sculptured from living models), and of that modern phase which he calls Romantic art, and in which nature appears only in the forms which the moral Universal assigns to it. I offer some samplings of his temper:[1]

> Here . . . has vanished that ideal beauty which [has sought to] replace its imperfect development by the blooming beauty of existence. Romantic Art no longer has for its aim this free vitality of actual existence, in its infinite calmness and submergence of the soul in the corporeal, nor even this *life*, as such, in its most precise significance, but turns its back upon this highest phase of beauty. Indeed, it interweaves its inner being with the accidentality of external organization, and allows unrestricted play room to the marked characteristics of the ugly. . . .

> In the Romantic, therefore, we have two worlds. The one is the spiritual realm [the Concrete Universal in the subjective existence], which is complete in itself—the soul, which finds its reconciliation within itself, and which now for the first time bends around the otherwise rectilinear repetition of genesis, destruction and renewal, to the true circle, to return-into-self, to the genuine Phoenix-life of the spirit. The other is the realm of the external, as such, which, shut out from a firmly cohering unity with the spirit, now becomes a wholly empirical actuality, respecting whose form the soul is unconcerned. . . .

[1] Translated by W. M. Bryant from the *Lectures in Aesthetics,* in the recent *Philosophy of Hegel,* edited by Carl J. Friedrich. (Modern Library.)

Thus though the soul is still destined to pass through the world, it no longer pursues merely worldly aims and undertakings. Rather, it has for its essential purpose and endeavor the inner struggle of man within himself, and his reconciliation with God, and brings into representation only personality and its conservation, together with appliances for the accomplishment of this end. . . .

Hegel is already at the point of abandoning nature, for the sake of realizing the modern society. But it is clear to him—he is in that degree still a Kantian—that this means the abandonment of poetry and art. His position is not too different from that of the "social" school of literary critics who hold on to prose fiction as an art while (virtually) they abandon poetry. My own feeling would be that in spite of the pressures of modern urban society, Hegel's example is not obligatory upon critics and artists; and that it is a very real question whether there is an art of fiction which has no poetry in it.

If I read Kant correctly, his is the more poetic soul, and the greater piety. I have come to think of him as the most radical and ultimate spokesman for poetry that we have had. We must approve his philosophical background. It was a British philosopher who woke him from his "dogmatic slumber," and conditioned him to the sort of intellectual scruple with which an empirical thinker faces the facts of life and of nature. The immediate consequence was one which lasted a painful while: the grim conviction that we must divide our effort between two sundered worlds, the free moral world which is wholly inner, and the natural world which is external but determinate and mechanical. (We know about the mechanical universe which Newton and his successors had furnished by Kant's time.) But finally he made the epoch-making discovery which seemed to bridge the abyss between them. To put this as simply as I can. There is no specific, singled-out event in nature which the understanding can regard as other than externally caused. But nature when we look hard refuses to be specific and single; it is everywhere itself, a dense "manifold of sense," a tissue of events whose effects are massive and intricate, beyond the grasp of the understanding. It is Kant's monumental achievement to have discerned how it is that nature nevertheless sometimes appears beautiful. These are the times when, filled with our own freedom and purpose, we find that nature too seems free and purposive. To be sure, Kant will not allow us to say that Nature's purpose is the same as ours, or that we quite understand it; we cannot claim, for example, that it is a moral purpose; but at least it seems sympathetic with our moral purpose. And the happiest consequences follow. The human kingdom and the natural kingdom appear like free and harmonious powers, collaborating with each other in dignity and peace; and in the sequel the poetic imagination is able to set up memorials of art which bear witness to their concord. Or if we require a bourgeois figure: we do not have to keep on feeling that the natural world is our alien habitation, for now it is our home. Or it is "our element." So it is not as if we had been deposited in a world in which we could not live with dignity unless we should build us a city and immure ourselves in a society.

Kant cites readily an instance or so of natural beauty. In a garden the foliage or the blossoms of the plants will answer insofar as the general profile is concerned to the gardener's geometrical Universal, yet their configuration in its profuse detail is much too intricate, and spontaneous-looking, to account for, and implies energies not used up by the Universal. It is as if the plants obeyed the law of their placement only to exhibit their own freedom beneath it the more luxuriantly. We have learned to think that this is just the right condition in which they will manifest their grace, or their beauty. And Kant has supplied the paradigm of natural beauty. (If there was anticipation of this paradigm, it was not on radical or philosophical grounds.) Nature seems to have no inclination to reject or even to resent the human Universal, for now obtains the condition of "freedom under the law," and its consequence of beauty. In these or similar terms the paradigm is recited nearly everywhere.

If this is natural beauty, what is poetry? Kant's view is simple, and for all except the new "symbolist" critics (who covet for poetry a "creativity" upon which there are to be no limits) it will be adequate: Poetry is the representation of natural beauty. The spectacular faculty of Imagination is its agent. Kant calls it the faculty of presentation, and says it is equivalent in the poet to Genius. The play between the understanding with its moral Universal on the one hand, and on the other hand Imagination presenting the purposive Concrete of nature, is unpredictable and inexhaustible. Coleridge, at least by the time of the *Biographia Literaria,* made a sort of official English version of Kant's view, and all critics are familiar with it. No statement is more studied than that sudden and enormous sentence at the bottom of Chapter XIV (in lieu of a great deal of promised text) in which the understanding and the imagination are paired ten times or so; the one which begins: "This power [Imagination], first put in action by the will and understanding and retained under their irremissive, though gentle and unnoticed, control (*laxis effertur habenis*) reveals itself in the balance or reconciliation of opposite or discordant qualities. . . ."

Kant hammered many times on the right way to construe the complex experience of beauty. He did not develop all the implications, nor provide systematic illustration. I will have to quote a small English poem which makes nature purposive with an almost excessive clarity, and indeed carries a tag of identification so pointed as to be embarrassing:

> The year's at the spring
> And day's at the morn;
> Morning's at seven;
> The hill-side's dew-pearled;
> The lark's on the wing;
> The snail's on the thorn:
> God's in his heaven—
> All's right with the world.

Little Pippa sings this song in passing, and a pair of guilty lovers recall their lost innocence and take to quarreling, like Adam and Eve after their Fall. Pippa's Universal is a feeling of joy, intense but diffused over every act and thought. (She is innocent, and this is her holiday from the silk mills.) She spends three lines dating the occasion very precisely, as Wordsworth might have identified his moment of illumination by way of his note-book, or even in the poem itself. Then come three details which constitute the Concrete: the hillside, the lark, the snail. A poem cannot and need not list all the details of the "manifold," only enough, and in variety startling enough, to make a fair sampling. We are given to understand that everything is joyful like Pippa, that all nature is animated in the morning light. And that would be the poem; except that she must conclude by putting in her theological Universal, in which she has been well instructed: the world rejoices because Pippa's God is now its God too, and he is in his heaven ordering all.

Kant would not have approved her tag. He was solicitous that the flowering of nature should not be subjected to the moral and theological Universals; for it could easily be that these are peculiar to the human understanding. It might be self-deception if we had wanted to discover that nature was moral and then proceeded to discover it. The nature-lover who studies actual nature, and the poet who imagines nature, must be on their guard against this possibility. The veteran critics of poetry today need no prompting to be on their guard.

Here is a passage in which the poet does not impose human responsibility upon nature quite so complacently. Shakespeare lived before the Romantics built up their great volume of business with nature, and in *Cymbeline* we observe his royal boys (who have been reared in the lap of nature, housed in a cave) as they stand by the grave of Fidele and improvise a funeral service. One of them says:

>   *With fairest flowers*
> *While summer lasts and I live here, Fidele,*
> *I'll sweeten thy sad grave; thou shalt not lack*
> *The flower that's like thy face, pale primrose, nor*
> *The azured harebell, like thy veins, no, nor*
> *The leaf of eglantine, whom not to slander,*
> *Outsweetened not thy breath: the ruddock would,*
> *With charitable bill, —O bill! sore-shaming*
> *Those rich-left heirs, that let their fathers lie*
> *Without a monument, —bring thee all this;*
> *Yea, and furred moss besides, when flowers are*
>   *none,*
> *To winter-ground thy corse.*

This is so handsome that we think, and perhaps we are not wrong, that Shakespeare has lent his own feeling to it. The flowers are gathered by human hands, and they resemble Fidele only in exterior features, not spiritually. But the speaker adds that if he were not bringing them, the red-breast (or ruddock) would; which might be crucial except that this sort of thing may be according to the folklore of red-breasts. (I find a small evidence in the new *Standard Dictionary of Folklore*.) It is an enticing idea all the same, for the poet goes on into an aside over the bird's "charitable bill" and offers the apostrophe beginning "O bill!" It is a mawkish moment of danger. But the other prince, the practical younger one, saves the situation when he scolds his brother for the speech:

> *Prithee, have done,*
> *And do not play in wench-like words with that*
> *Which is so serious.*

And Shakespeare has put up his guard, his decent Kantian reservation.

It would be wrong to give the impression that in a poem, necessarily, the intellectual Universal has always disappeared from sight and now exists only in the Concrete. It is my impression that as often as not a poem will recite its two versions, side by side. Thus Portia, commending mercy, explains that mercy does not come by compulsion but spontaneously or by grace: its quality is "not strained," or, as we would say, "unconstrained." That is the moral Universal. Then comes the poetic consummation. As if this abstract talk of the Universal might not be quite intelligible, she adds, "It droppeth as the gentle rain from heaven/Upon the place beneath." And in the following passage the poet Yeats, who likes to show the strain of his intellectual ideas, looks hard at his metaphor or Concrete before he accepts it for his Universal:

> *Some moralist or mythological poet*
> *Compares the solitary soul to a swan;*
> *I am satisfied with that,*
> *Satisfied if a troubled mirror show it,*
> *Before that brief gleam of its life be gone,*
> *An image of its state:*

The wings half spread for flight,
The breast thrust out in pride.
Whether to play or to ride
Those winds that clamor of approaching night.

But it may be otherwise. By a *tour de force* in the metaphorical style, which for more reasons than one we are apt to call "metaphysical," the Universal of a poem may be wholly translated into a natural image, or a series of them, and never expressed in the abstract language of the understanding at all; as in that Shakespearian sonnet which begins the first of three images with "That time of year thou mayst in me behold."

Probably it is normal, when the Universal receives a metaphorical or natural image, for the Universal to come first; tenor precedes vehicle, as we say it today. But we must observe that this order may be quite reversed. A natural object or confirmation strikes our attention because it seems significant of more than mechanical effect, and we proceed to equate it metaphorically with the appropriate human Universal. In this case we start with nature and humanize it; in the other case we started with the human Universal and naturalized it. How, for example, shall the modern poet explain his depression over the late evening that has not even the dignity of a sunset sky? It is "spread out against the sky/Like a patient etherized upon the table"; as if it might not survive the operation. Kant himself observes that the poem may begin at either end of the process. He quotes "a certain poet" observing the sunrise and letting it lead into his own moral reflection:

The sun arose
As calm from virtue springs.

The observer does not stop with the meteorological fact but finds, says Kant, that it "diffuses in the mind a multitude of sublime and restful feelings and a boundless prospect of a joyful future, to which no expression measured by a definite concept [*i.e.*, keeping to the tenor] completely attains."

Marvell combines with his sophistication or worldliness an extravagant love of gardens and nature. He often begins a metaphor with a natural object, and sometimes humanizes it almost absurdly. But his guard is up, too, and his tone is therefore apt to be waggish. Thus his Mower addresses the Glowworms in one poem:

> *Ye living lamps, by whose dear light*
> *The nightingale does sit so late,*
> *And studying all the summer night*
> *Her matchless songs does meditate;*
>
> *Ye country comets, that portend*
> *No war nor prince's funeral,*
> *Shining unto no higher end*
> *Than to presage the grass's fall.*

His famous "Garden" poem has burlesque moments along with its proper beauties; he pretends to picture the Garden as his preferred and adequate element, supplying him with natural satisfactions which are precisely of the same kind as those he could have had in the human society:

> *No white nor red was ever seen*
> *So amorous as this lovely green.*
> *Fond lovers, cruel as their flame,*
> *Cut in these trees their mistresses name:*
> *Little, alas, they know, or heed,*
> *How far these beauties hers exceed!*
> *Fair trees, wheresoe'er your barks I wound*
> *No name shall but your own be found.*

He is more direct than metaphorical in "Bermudas"

where the colonists recite the kindness of the natural element which God has given them.

> *He gave us this eternal spring,*
> *Which here enamels everything;*
> *And sends the fowls to us in care,*
> *On daily visits through the air.*
> *He hangs in shades the orange bright,*
> *Like golden lamps in a green night.*
> *And does in the pomgranates close*
> *Jewels more rich than Ormus shows.*
> *He makes the figs our mouths to meet;*
> *And throws the melons at our feet.*
> *But apples plants of such a price,*
> *No tree could ever bear them twice.*
> *With cedars, chosen by his hand,*
> *From Lebanon, he stores the land,*
> *And makes the hollow seas that roar,*
> *Proclaim the ambergris on shore.*
> *He cast (of which we rather boast)*
> *The gospels pearl upon our coast.*
> *And in these rocks for us did frame*
> *A temple, where to sound his name.*

The purpose of nature is identified completely with the care of Providence. Kant would not have found it according to the canon. The best we can say of it is that the colonists sing this naive song as they row their boat, so that there is drama in it.

Wallace Stevens has written a poem expressly under the title of "The Motive for Metaphor," and I think Kant would have acecpted it as a stylized but competent variation upon his own view:

> *You like it under the trees in autumn,*
> *Because everything is half dead.*
> *The wind moves like a cripple among the leaves*
> *And repeats words without meaning.*

In the same way, you were happy in spring,
With the half colors of quarter-things,
The slightly brighter sky, the melting clouds,
The single bird, the obscure moon—

The obscure moon lighting an obscure world
Of things that would never be quite expressed,
Where you yourself were never quite yourself
And did not want nor have to be.

Desiring the exhilaration of changes:
The motive for metaphor, shrinking from
The weight of primary noon,
The A B C of being,

The ruddy temper, the hammer
Of red and blue, the hard sound—
Steel against intimation—the sharp flash,
The vital, arrogant, fatal, dominant X.

That is to say, I think, something like the following. "You like metaphor in the autumn, because you cannot express yourself, except to say that the wind cannot express itself either. You like it in the spring, because instead of trying to express what you feel then, you can speak of how the obscure moon lights an obscure world. You like it because it is exhilarating, and alternative to the dreary searching of your own mind for the meaning of your state. [There must be many a moral Universal seeking its poetry though it is no better than a moral feeling; so much of the moral life turns on feeling, and on half-successful reflection, and can scarcely ever be satisfied except with a poetic expression or its homely equivalent.] The moral Universal is intolerably harsh and simple, when you phrase it, not equal to what you want it to mean, and in fact it is the 'vital, arrogant, fatal, dominant X'; it is inexpressive, like the sign of an unknown quantity." So much more visible, more audible, more tangible, better focussed for the senses, are the behaviors of nature which the poet can draw upon because they are expressive. This poem makes an important remark in a very casual manner, and many of us will already be possessed of the notion, as I imagine, that no poet has written more verse about the understanding of poetry than Stevens has done, unless it was Wordsworth. If it had not been Richard Blackmur who wrote recently about Stevens as a poet not only dandiacal but unphilosophical, I should have boggled at both ascriptions, and thought that Blackmur's own guard was down, most unaccountably. But it *was* Blackmur, and Blackmur as a critic is so far from having an impediment in his vision or his speech that he excels other critics in the latitude of his contexts, so that I dare say there are intimations in the one about Stevens which amount to the right qualifications; amount to them in a measure if not in full.

The longest quotation of verse in Kant's own writing is from the poem by Frederick the Great written in French: "sur les vaines terreurs de la mort et les frayeurs d'une autre vie." Although Kant had translated the verse into German for his own text, our English editor and translator supplies it in the original language:[2]

> *Oui, finissons sans trouble et mourons sans regrets,*
> *En laissant l'univers comblé de nos bienfaits.*
> *Ainsi l'astre du jour au bout de sa carrière,*
> *Repànd sur l'horizon une douce lumière;*
> *Et les derniers rayons qu'il darde dans les airs,*
> *Sont les derniers soupirs qu'il donne à l'univers.*

The King at the end of his full life is metaphorically

[2] *Kant's Critique of Judgment,* translated and edited by J. H. Bernard. Second edition, London, 1914. (Macmillan.)

represented by the sun taking a last look round upon the world he has illuminated before he goes down. That is all, but the sun's moment is a rich one. Kant comments that here

> the great King . . . quickens his rational Idea of a cosmopolitan disposition at the end of life by an attribute which the Imagination (in remembering all the pleasures of a beautiful summer day that are recalled at its close by a serene evening) associates with that representation, and which excites a number of sensations and secondary representations for which no expression is found.

No expression is found in the tenor for the sensations and secondary representations, which therefore are assigned to the vehicle to express. Is it that no expression *can* be found in the tenor, that the language of feeling is too poor to allow of that? I take it so. And if it is so, then Kant in effect is saying precisely what Mr. Cleanth Brooks as a modern critic has been saying to his own public over and over: that "there is no other way" for language to express what it wants to express without having recourse to metaphor; without going to the Concrete of nature for its analogy. I cannot think that Kant would have repudiated his implication, but that he would have stated it with his usual boldness—if he could have foreseen the difficult passages, and the *impasses*, which the subsequent course of literary criticism would encounter, and the need of developing his own principles most specifically.

The understanding of poetry which I have attributed to Kant in these notes is less than the whole of that philosopher's deliverance; but I think I have indicated the burden of it. I have ventured to furnish him with a word which perhaps will describe in our time, and for our critics, the way of the imagination in giving objective or Concrete existence to the homeless moral Universal. The word is metaphor, and Kant makes no particular use of it. He has not supplied poetic studies detailed enough, or in number enough, to have fixed on it for his regular word. But it would seem a decisive word for his understanding of poetry; it gives us the sense of nature accepting the Universal readily into its infinite system, and lending to it what metaphysical sanction is possible.

Many critics of our time, starting let us say with Richards and coming on now at least to Professor Wimsatt, have uttered bold ideas about metaphor, and I have not gone far beyond some of them. To say "metaphor" tirelessly, with brutal repetition, is one militant way of defending nature as the element to which the Universal is referred, and therefore the element to which poetry has to look. I think the defenders of poetry would not mind saying that they are not prepared to abandon nature, because that would be the abandonment of metaphor, which in turn would mean the abandonment of poetry; which, when they have weighed it, would be a serious abridgment of the range of the human experience. The alternative to sticking by nature and poetry is to follow Hegel's view that the moderns are now so far advanced with their perfectly specific and practicable Universals, their faith in these is so sure, and the conduct of them fulfills so completely the range of our demands, that nothing remains for the human spirit but to put all its strength into society and politics. My critics are scarcely going to agree with that.

But critics are notoriously impressionable, as perhaps it is their business to be; and every day I have a new sense of the wide spread of that Hegelian type of modernity. I can liken myself modestly to Arnold in the respect that, though I am not an inspector of schools, I have done a long turn as a schoolmaster of poetry, and even acquired some professional anecdotes of my own. The latest one is not ten days old. A former pupil, after spending several years in business employment, came to me to say that he wished now to go on to a graduate school for further studies in literature; and to ask if I might tell him at what university he might find teachers whose interest was concentrated upon modern fiction, therefore upon the social sensibility. As for the teachers of poetry, who abound in the universities, he explained that in his business life he had been so impressed with his social responsibility that he could no longer bear to read works in that old-fashioned art. And though I was shocked by his apostasy, I was not so shocked but that I was able with a straight face to tell him what he wanted to know, so far as my information permitted. I assured him with all sincerity that the masters of morality nowadays were indeed the sociologists, who understood the moral pressures of modern society, and that among the ablest sociologists, and even among the most learned sociologists, were many literary critics whose professional occupation was with fiction.

I have also had experiences showing how a certain practical kind of religiosity, like practical morality when it possesses us, is capable of getting in between the soul and its reception of poetry and literature. This is when the soul is a timid soul and prefers the security of dogma to the dreadful facts of life and the pusillanimous dialectic by which poetry deals with them. But I do not wish to recite these experiences; they are not pretty stories and even the humor of them is painful. I remark that the poet's theology is metaphorical, and the poet knows it is metaphorical, and insists like Keats in holding by a rule of Negative Capability,—which is not a Kantian phrase, but sounds like one, and might have been one if Kant, once more, had elaborated his views further than he did. By this rule a theological representation is in terms of our understanding of this world, and though it is hopeful it is far from determining about any other world. And if people are young enough and adventurous enough to go to college, they ought not to cheat themselves of those beautiful yet mortal representations offered them in literature.

To go only a little further. What is, characteristically, the religious faith of a poet? Or, if strictly speaking he has nothing quite orthodox to show under that head, what is the sort of faith which he does have? Kant knew that faith, though chiefly he lived by his strong religious faith; which was other-worldly yet of extreme Protestant severity, quite declining to let the imagination of this world give it a form. I should say that we might call the poet's piety a "natural" piety, his gift being for finding the natural world not merely mechanical but hospitable to the moral Universals. In literature this piety is recorded perhaps in that later mood of Wordsworth's, arrived at during the years between the other-worldly opening of the "Ode on Intimations of Immortality" and its more modest and slightly sad conclusion. But, regardless of what might have been Kant's professional feelings, I would like to borrow here from another philosopher. The poet's faith, I should say, is that this is "the best of all possible worlds"; inasmuch as it is not possible for imagination to acquaint us with any other world. It is a horrid as well as a beautiful world, but without the horror we should never focus the beauty; without death there would be no relish for life; without danger, no courage; without savagery, no gentleness; and without the background of our frequent ignominy, no human dignity and pride. (These are excellent and rather Hegelian commonplaces.) Wordsworth at the beginning of his Ode advanced the ancient doctrine of metempsychology, without remarking that there is provided traditionally, betwixt the residence of the soul in one world and its residence in another world, a Lethean bath to bring forgetfulness of that nature which the soul has just lived with; in order that it may adapt to whatever nature may be next in order. To the theologian the poet might want to say, One world at a time.

Most of Kant's understanding of poetry—if we except the middle section of the work which is concerned with the sublime—is devoted to that high moment in which we suddenly perceive what we may call the Epiphany of Beauty. It uses up the whole of a poetry, with the Universals of the mind deploying against the natural metaphors, and then our recognition of the consequence, to create this show. Kant's understanding therefore chooses to regard poetry as a single and powerful though complicated action; and that is the kind of view which is deeply coveted by the modern critics. It is a complete view—expect for one reservation which is anticlimactic, and a little embarrassing, and after all not exactly trifling.

Kant's description is of a poetic phrase, or passage, or of a short poem; it is the description of a lyrical effect—if we can divorce that term from the idea of music, which does not come under Kant's notice as essential—or of a moment of illumination; it is the soul of poetry caught briefly, but completely and characteristically.

And yet—what are we to say about long poems? about philosophical poems, or epics, or poetic narratives, or poetic dramas? It cannot often be that the action focuses upon a single metaphorical or metaphysical moment. The chances are, overwhelmingly, that the moral Universal in such cases is a considerable and organized sequence of intellectual ideas, or of historical events, embodied for action and working themselves out; or, it is just possible, not clearly embodied, and only talking themselves out; and the best we can hope for, as Kantians, is that there are many happy metaphorical transformations, or little poetries, in the course of the poem, and perhaps a conclusion suited to the faith of a poet. This order of poetry will be much more put together, or synthetic, than the lyric, and more capable, indeed more demanding, of being separated by analysis into its primary parts. A different thing.

And a different story for critics, though not altogether. With poetry of this sort I have sometimes been at pains to defend the rights of the intellectuals (the moralists or religionists) to isolate the ideas and discuss them on their intellectual merits; inasmuch as the ideas are surely in the poetry; and ideas demand discussion by intellectuals, the very best intellectuals that will offer. This is a poetry that can be taken apart. And yet if it is really a poetry it cannot be hurt; and Kantians can come back to the whole poetry and see what is poetical about it.

JOHN CROWE RANSOM *was born in Pulaski, Tennessee, in 1888. After attending Vanderbilt University and Oxford (as a Rhodes scholar), he served on the faculty of Vanderbilt from 1914 to 1937. Since that time he has taught at Kenyon College, where he also edits the* Kenyon Review. *He has published four volumes of verse:* Poems about God, Chills and Fever, Two Gentlemen in Bonds, *and* Selected Poems; *and three of prose:* God Without Thunder, The World's Body, *and* The New Criticism. *In 1951 Mr. Ransom received the Bollingen Prize for Poetry and the Russell Loines Memorial Fund Prize from the National Institute of Arts and Letters.*

THIS BOOK *was set on the Linotype in Janson, an excellent example of the influential and sturdy Dutch types that prevailed in England prior to the development by William Caslon of his own designs, which he evolved from these Dutch faces. Of Janson himself little is known except that he was a practising typefounder in Leipzig during the years 1660 to 1687. Composed, printed, and bound by* THE COLONIAL PRESS INC., *Clinton, Massachusetts. Cover design by* BRADBURY THOMPSON.